STRONGER
Every
SINGLE
Day

How to Defeat Heartbreak and
Have Fulfillment While Living Single

JESSICA S. YARBROUGH
Foreword By: Pastor Sheryl Banks

WWW.SELFPUBLISHN30DAYS.COM

Published by Self Publish -N- 30 Days

Printed in the United States of America

ISBN: 978-1-69563-407-7 1. Nonfiction 2. Inspirational Stronger Every Single Day: How to Defeat Heartbreak and Have Fulfillment While Living Single

This book is dedicated to singles who have undergone traumatic experiences or disappointments in life and in relationships. The Father saw your tears, heard your silent cries and placed a burden in my heart just for you.

Table of Contents

Acknowledgments

I am grateful that God provided this avenue to share His Good News. I want to acknowledge my parents, Apostle Larry W. and Co-Pastor Jessie Yarbrough, for laying a solid and Godly foundation. And for your unwavering love and support, thank you, Mom and Dad.

I am forever thankful for my pastors, Apostle Craig Banks, DD, and Pastor Sheryl Banks, DD, for believing in me and for pushing me to purpose. Thank you for all your Kingdom deposits.

To Apostle Alphonso Montgomery, Evangelist Patsy Robinson, Prophetess Vera Jackson, and Minister Angula Davis: Thank you for hearing God concerning me.

To Sacia, Merely Meredith, Eddie L. and Eddie F.: Thank you for putting up with all my random midday brainstorming.

To Carla: Thank you for our conversations. You inspired me to step out on faith and pursue my next level of purpose.

I am the Alpha and the Omega,
the First and the Last,
and What you see,
write in a book and send it…
Revelation 1:11a, NKJV

Foreword

I can remember vividly when Jessica started visiting our church, Canaan Christian Center. After a few visits, she called and made an appointment to meet with us about becoming a member. She had a lot of fact-finding questions. I can recall thinking, "She is very young, but serious, business minded, and very conscientious in her decision-making process in finding a church home!"

Fast forward: Jessica has now been an integral part of the ministry at Canaan for several years. During this time, we have observed her personal and spiritual growth as a young woman in ministry.

It is my opinion that this book is an answer to the silent screams of countless individuals who are unhappy, unfulfilled, and are not in a place of wholeness. There are many who have been heartbroken, abused, and misused. They have become "stuck on the ropes" in a place where they have been unable to move their lives forward to the "center of the ring."

In this book, Jessica masterfully lays out, in "Boxer-Training" Analysis, a strategic daily guide for your personal training that repositions you to win. It has easy life applications, and most importantly is scripturally sound.

So get ready, for you are about to embark on a journey that will set you free to live your best life in healing and wholeness, and to stand in the winners' circle!

Pastor Sheryl Banks DD
Canaan Christian Center
Pine Bluff, Arkansas

Introduction

W elcome to training camp. Training camps usually consist of accelerated physical fitness objectives that challenge an individual's motivation, physical endurance, and desire to succeed. My job is to stretch each of you to the limit in your thinking, perspectives, and spiritual maturation. The goal of this training institution is to ensure that you walk in all that God has ordained for you in this single season and beyond.

Every perfect gift comes from above. If we take a moment and reflect on God and His perfection, I am certain that we can think of a plethora of qualities that He has, all of which we should long to display. Scripture tells us that everything that God created in the beginning was good.

In His supernatural and infinite wisdom, God designed the family unit with us in mind. His goal was to set in motion a strong family institution, consisting of men, women and children, thereby creating strong communities and an even stronger body of Christ. However, with the infusion of man's imperfections into daily life and the family structure, it leaves so much to be desired in the hearts of millions, particularly singles.

Satan's goal was and is to weaken and ultimately destroy the sacred family structure and he seeks to do so by various means. One way he does so is by discouraging individuals who have experienced failed dating relationships and marriages in such a way that they continue to live a life of pain and dysfunction.

Like so many others, I have been a target of Satan's tactics in that I have survived the excruciating effects of heartbreak and was once in a state of emotional, mental and spiritual paralysis. The weapon formed, but it did not prosper. Thanks to God, I was able to overcome those challenging circumstances and so will you.

This book will serve as an instrument to reach the hearts of those who have been scarred by failed relationships, yet who desire to overcome the effects of those failures. The techniques that I share are not just things that I heard about, but they are strategies that I personally employed to dig out of the ravine of despair. During the time I experienced the challenges, about which you will read, I did not realize that God would birth a new dimension of passion and concern within me for singles.

I am living proof that all things work together for our good. Ultimately, I believe this process of overcoming heartbreak was God-ordained so that I can be a conduit of healing to share truths and revelations with those that will receive. It did not happen overnight for me, but once I made up my mind to go after healing and fulfillment, I became and am still becoming stronger every SINGLE day!

I pray that your heart is open. So, while you read each page, imagine that you are a boxer and I am your trainer. It's time to suit up and train. Remember that in the process of getting into shape that there are moments of discomfort because every part of your body must be challenged, even those parts that you have forgotten exist. I am confident that upon your completion of this book, that you will be stronger mentally, emotionally, and spiritually than you were before. So, get your gloves on! We have a fight to win!

I pray that from His glorious, unlimited resources He will empower you with inner strength through His Spirit. Then Christ will make His home in your hearts as you trust in Him. Your roots will grow down into God's love and keep you strong. And may you have the power to understand, as all God's people should, how wide, how long, how high, and how deep His love is. May you experience the love of Christ, though it is too great to understand fully. Then you will be made complete with all the fullness of life and power that comes from God.

Ephesians 3:16–19, NLT

THE WARM-UP

Ladies and gentlemen, thank you for showing up today.
Let's get started!

Training Day 1

Heartbreak Happens

O ne of my favorite movies is Rocky IV, part of an original film series. All of the films were written and directed by the one and only Sylvester Stallone. Rocky IV stands out to me because after Rocky Balboa had experienced success and had become the heavyweight boxing champion, he would have a life-changing experience that would ultimately challenge his physical strength, mental toughness, and his ability to pick up the fragments of a broken heart in order to fight on.

Rocky's best friend, Apollo Creed, was killed while fighting an over-sized Russian opponent in an exhibition boxing match. It is easy to see the passion and fury in Rocky's eyes as he held his dying friend in his arms. At that point, he had a decision to make. Would he crawl into a cave and die, or would he pick up the pieces and train like never before so that he could defeat the culprit that so coldly took the life of an innocent fighter?

If you watch the film, you will see that Rocky schedules a fight with the Russian to defend his friend's honor. Rocky then goes to Russia and trains for the fight using snow, mountains, and other things that would seem to be obstacles, to his advantage in order to reach maximum physical shape. Not only did he have to train in an unfamiliar environment, but he had to do so while thousands of miles away from his family, friends, and fans.

The Russian was much taller, had a longer reach, trained in a state-of-the-art facility, and used the unfair advantage of steroids. One would think that Rocky and the Russian should not have been in the same weight class. Nonetheless, in his bout against the Russian, Rocky stretches himself to the limit, taking blows and giving them until he finally secures the knock-out and wins over a hostile crowd.

When training for most sports, one must first gain an understanding of the sport itself, such as the rules of the game, what it takes to win, and the most common ways to be disqualified. Upon gleaning an understanding of the ins and outs, one must then prepare his or her body to meet the demands of competition. Boxing is a combat sport that dates back to the ancient Egyptian civilizations and is likely one of the oldest martial arts in the history of combat.[1] Boxers undergo extensive training so that they may be contenders in the ring with opponents that are of equal weight.

Have you ever noticed how in shape most boxers are? Studies show that boxing training programs are positively linked to physical fitness and technical performance effectiveness in that they help to improve agility and quickness, core (abdomen) strength, as well as cardio and muscle development. These programs also enhance technical skills, such as offensive and defensive techniques.[2] When engaged in boxing training, one may feel that the skipping rope and medicine ball rotational throws are totally unrelated to perfecting one's craft as a boxer. Yet, each step is crucial in order to reach maximum ability and to be an ultimate contender.

If you are taking the time to read this, then chances are you or someone you know has been in the ring with heartbreak and experienced some of its uppercuts, jabs and blows. It rears its ugly head in a myriad of ways, whether through childhood traumas, adolescent secrets, or adulthood difficulties. Rejection is an all too familiar version of heartbreak and many may find a commonality with rejection through job loss, divorce, or a painful breakup.

It is not unusual for today's single to have experienced the reality of an aching heart, whether it resulted from a marriage that never materialized, a failed marriage, or from extended periods of isolation and loneliness. Sometimes it may seem that heartbreak plays as dirty as the Russian did when he killed an innocent fighter and when he used illegal steroids against Rocky. Rest assured that you are not alone, and it is OK to have experienced the feelings of a broken heart.

Men and women alike understand the overwhelming grief that accompanies heartache, even if the display of such grief is polar opposite in nature. Sadness, despair, anger, resentment, unforgiveness, bitterness, confusion, fear, anxiety, and depression are but a few emotions that tend to form tributaries from the cesspool of heartache. I know first-hand. Each person can appreciate his own bouts in the ring with heartbreak. Something that seems so miniscule to one may feel like the end of the world to another.

> **Rejection is an all too familiar version of heartbreak.**

Before the Bout

I had an amazing childhood and was reared in a home with loving parents and two older brothers that I couldn't live without. However, there are a few challenging moments that are so easy to recall. For example, I remember that while in elementary school during physical education class, the coach split us into two teams for an exhilarating game of kick-ball. Of course, the winning team would tout bragging rights until we played again.

I can recall vividly that the team captains were eager to select the people that they knew would help seal the win. In my mind, I knew I was athletic and had the ability to kick the ball over the fence. But I was one of the last ones to be picked to a team. Almost immediately a large chip formed on my shoulder and I knew I had something to prove.

When it was finally my turn to kick, I gave it all I possibly could, and the ball sailed across the playground. I relished in the "ooohs" and "ahhhs." From that day forward, I was one of the first to be picked to various teams during P.E., of course.

That example may seem extremely lighthearted, and I dare not over-magnify the experience. Nonetheless, it carries significance because it developed a trajectory in my life and a mindset to prove to others what I had to offer. To this day, I can recall how I felt while waiting to be picked by a team: I entertained thoughts of fear, worry, and self-doubt. All these feelings raced through my mind while hoping that one of the team captains would see the good in me. Perhaps you have experienced something at some point in your life that you are able to recall which ignited feelings of self-doubt or insecurities.

As I matriculated in school and in life, I always had to be the best at whatever I did. Oftentimes, I placed undue pressure on myself to increase in skill, knowledge, and expertise in any endeavor that I set out to accomplish. I became a winner at heart. Sometimes my friends would loathe to challenge me in any friendly competition because they felt that I was overly competitive.

As years passed, I developed the nerve to begin dating. My parents left no stone unturned with my brothers and me. They instilled the Word of God in us at young ages. As a result, we knew what to do and what not to do, whether we followed the instructions or not. I had given my life to Christ at age 12, and at age 19, I delivered my first sermon. While I had my share of struggles, temptations, and shortcomings, my sincere desire was to please the Lord and make my family proud.

As a young adult, I met a few nice guys to date. Some in the church and some not. Ultimately, my spiel was the same: "I'm not having sex with you." Of course, the response was usually, "Oh, I'm cool with that. I respect your decision." Whether that was an honest answer, or a politically correct answer has yet to be determined (I vouch for the latter in some cases).

> **I entertained thoughts of fear, worry, and self-doubt.**

Countless times, I would get involved, develop feelings, and then disappointment would soon follow. For me, it seemed that many of my significant others were lured away by other women hanging in the balance for the right opportunity to send them a winning salacious signal. This happened over and over. I began to evaluate whether my standards were too high and unrealistic. Whatever the reasons, I felt like a loser.

You may be asking the same question that I began to ask myself:

"What's wrong with me?" I began to question my self-worth, my appearance, and my desirability. We all have our own set of flaws; yet, as I reflected, I knew that in each relationship, I was honest and loyal with the best of intentions, even if I did not do everything right. I was not street savvy, so I did not know how to play games.

In life, I discovered that there are countless reasons why relationships do not last. All the time, it is not because of unfaithfulness, abuse, or because either individual is a bad person or has poor character. Sometimes two people are just not compatible. Whatever the reason relationships end, it can still hurt. If we choose, we can examine our past relationships and with crystal clarity, we can identify warning signs, prophetic voices, and every red flag that flashed before our eyes because hindsight is usually 20/20.

As Christians, we must remember that just because we meet someone who is spiritually mature or operating in spiritual gifts, that does not make that person our ideal spouse or soulmate. It is important to realize that people are people. Yet, most of us have had moments in which we were unable to heed the warnings when they were given because our emotions were much stronger than our discernment.

How Heartbreak Works

Repetitive heartbreak is highly likely to occur when individuals do not receive healing for themselves before entering subsequent relationships. That individual will risk reinjuring themselves and will injure another person because a broken heart does not have the capacity to love the way it is intended to love.

I believe that many times, God seeks to spare our hearts from unnecessary pain, but in our haste and lack of sensitivity to the voice of God, we make executive decisions that cause heartache in the end. Consequently, true communion with God is of paramount importance for singles so that we can hear God's voice and obey His instructions above the cries and desires of our flesh.

Heartbreak can be especially daunting for the person who made an honest attempt to seek God for direction and confirmation concerning a mate, only to experience a failed marriage or a break-up. It can be very discouraging and confusing to think that you have heard from God concerning a person or a matter, only for the situation to end in the exact opposite fashion. I have several colorful memories of the instances that my heart was ripped apart. There were times that I convinced myself that I had sought God concerning the relationships that I would enter, only for them to end in a whirlwind of sadness and déjà vu. In those moments, I felt forsaken, lost, confused and ready to give up on dating and relationships.

Regardless of the avenue through which your heartbreak has come, it is real to you. Studies show that emotional pain feels much like physical pain. According to Dr. Guy Winch, a licensed psychologist, heartbreak activates similar mechanisms in the brain to those activated when we experience physical pain. For example, functional magnetic resonance imaging (fMRI) studies of brain activity have found that heartbreak activates the same mechanisms in the brain that are activated when addicts are withdrawing from substances such as cocaine.

Some have even reported a literal ache in their chest after heartbreak. These symptoms impact our ability to focus, think and function. If your heart has ever been crushed from the loss of a loved one, a failed relationship, or any traumatic event or disappointing experience, then you can likely identify with these findings.

From another physiological standpoint, heart failure, by broad definition, is a progressive clinical syndrome in which the heart fails to pump sufficient blood to the body due to a functional or structural cardiac disorder.[3] Without a healthy heart, one would struggle to have a healthy body. Without the proper medical attention, a heart failure patient's quality of life would diminish. Many times, this leads to bouts of depression. While more research is necessary to determine an actual link between depression and mortality in heart failure patients, some studies have revealed that depression predicted higher mortality and faster decline in patients' health status.[4]

Compare those physiological findings to the psychological and emotional aspect of our lives. When we experience heartbreak, other areas of life are affected, which can decrease our quality of life. Other areas that may be affected as a result of heartbreak may include one's self-confidence, faith in God, or the motivation to pursue purpose.

My goal is to assist you and offer the emotional, spiritual, and moral support necessary to nurse you back to health. Yes, heartbreak happens, but thank God, it does not have to win. Your name has finally been called and you're on the winning team. It's time to step into the ring and knock heartbreak out for the count!

Christ's Position on Heartbreak

In the Word of God, the Old Testament prophecy from the Book of Isaiah was fulfilled in Luke 4:18. Isaiah had given a foreshadowing of the coming King. In the New Testament, when Jesus returned to Galilee after being tempted by the devil for 40 days, He began teaching in the synagogues. He then visited Nazareth, his hometown, and taught there. At that point, Jesus made it known what part of His mission would be.

The Spirit of the Lord is upon Me,
because He has anointed Me to preach the gospel to the
poor; He has sent Me to heal the brokenhearted.
Luke 4:18a, NKJV

These words had been spoken in the Old Testament by the Prophet Isaiah of what was to come. Jesus would come to preach the Gospel of salvation to mankind. He would give His life to redeem mankind and wash away our sins by the shedding of His blood. His shedding of blood does not stop at saving our souls so that we may inherit eternal life and escape hell. It is His will that we live an abundant life on earth, full of joy, happiness, health, and prosperity.

Therefore, if your heart is or has ever been broken, Jesus came with you in mind. God wants to heal your broken hearts, emotions, and even your painful memories. A beautiful and reassuring fact is that everything we need in life has already been provided for us through Christ. We must simply access those things by faith (which will be discussed more in depth on Training Day 6).

When Jesus was nailed to the cross, He bore the sins of the whole world so that we would be redeemed back to God. Forgiveness was provided to us even before our parents and grandparents were born. Not only did Jesus defeat sin when He was resurrected from the dead, but He also defeated sickness, disease, mental illness, poverty, and yes, a broken heart. Thus, Christ has

> **He also defeated sickness, disease, mental illness, poverty, and yes, a broken heart.**

17

already defeated heartbreak and He came to heal yours. Because Christ has won, we are winners in Him.

> He personally carried our sins in His body on the cross [willingly offering Himself on it, as on an altar of sacrifice], so that we might die to sin [becoming immune from the penalty and power of sin] and live for righteousness; for by His wounds you [who believe] have been healed.
> **I Peter 2:24, AMP**

Notice that the scripture indicates that our healing has already taken place. By His wounds, we who believe **were** healed. Before we were born, Christ's redemptive work on the cross provided the answer to believing prayer. We must receive it by faith. You may ask: "How do I receive it by faith?" Just accept that your heart has been healed, even if it does not feel like it at times. Understand that we are children of God, which makes us heirs to His promises, and joint heirs with Christ. God has freely given us all things and just as Jesus is entitled to everything His Father has, so are we. We must access those things by faith.

For the purposes of this illustration, consider your employment. Most of us go to work day after day, being confident that we will be compensated on payday. We actually go to work by faith because anything could happen and prevent us from getting paid.

Sometimes, we arrive at work tired or even sick, but we know that our feelings do not alter our status or responsibilities as an employee. So even if we do not feel like being an employee, if we maintain our position, we will receive a paycheck on a certain day. We may even subconsciously begin to feel better the closer we get to payday because we know that it is coming. Still, the fruition of payday is not based on a feeling. It is based upon facts. Those facts include that if we do our job, we are entitled to a paycheck.

Accepting your healing for a broken heart is very similar. You may not feel like your heart has been healed, but if you believe in Christ's redemptive work, you shall receive what you ask of Him. After you have accepted the truth of the matter, that you are healed and that your broken heart has been defeated on the cross, then you must walk out the process of your healing to receive the total manifestation of what God has already provided.

The fight was already fixed before you arrived on the scene. You just need to do your part and change your stance to that of a winner. You must ensure that your entire being (mind, soul and body) lines up with what your spirit knows: that heartbreak is already defeated, and you are victorious.

So, use the same mindset that you use in showing up for work and maintaining your position. If you can have faith to believe that a paycheck will manifest after two weeks, then do not underestimate God's power and willingness to bless you. The advantage of the Kingdom is that you do not have to work to earn the healing because Jesus provided our healing on the cross. Our job is to bring our lives into configuration with what God has provided in the Spirit realm.

You are a citizen of the Kingdom of God. You are a winner! Keep retraining your mind, soul and body, regardless of how you feel, and you will receive that manifested healing. We are about to embark upon an exciting excursion. As we prepare to bring our lives into alignment with what Christ has provided, we must whip ourselves into shape by adjusting our thinking and our posture. If you are ready to take this journey with me, then by all means, keep reading!

Training Day 2

In the Beginning...

Have you ever wondered why bad things happen to good people? Have you also wondered why so many single Christians struggle with singleness and it seems that it is so difficult to meet the right person? I am sure that you have. Well, the Lord provided a revelation to me in order to enlighten my understanding.

Most of us are familiar with the story of Adam and Eve. Prior to the creation of man, you will learn in the Book of Genesis Chapter 1, that God created the heavens and the earth, and everything was good. He then called for the earth to bring forth living creatures and it was so. He made wild beasts and domestic animals. When God created the waters, He spoke to the waters and commanded that they bring forth living creatures, fish and everything that lives under water, and He approved it. When God prepared to make man, He said:

Let Us [Father, Son, and Holy Spirit] make man in Our image, after Our likeness, and let them have complete authority over the fish of the sea, the birds of the air, the [tame] beasts, and over all of the earth, and over everything that creeps upon the earth.
Genesis 1:26, AMPC

In Genesis Chapter 2, God planted a garden toward the east in Eden, which means delight, and that is where He placed Adam, who was given dominion over all creation on earth. Adam was not just placed on earth to be a gardener. He was to reign as ruler on earth. If he was created in God's image and likeness, then he would be able to speak, and the winds and seas obey him. Scripture states that God had also made every tree that is pleasant to the sight or to be desired for food. The tree of life was in the center of the garden, along with the tree of the knowledge of good and evil. The Lord God put Adam in the Garden of Eden to tend and to keep it as part of his responsibilities as ruler.

> **If he was created in God's image and likeness, then he would be able to speak, and the winds and seas obey him.**

Some argue that God created a failing situation for Adam by placing him in the garden with the commands to not eat of the tree. To the contrary, God made man in His image and likeness, but He also gave man the ability to think for himself and to choose to love Him.[5] God commanded Adam, saying:

Of every tree of the garden you may freely eat; but of the tree of the knowledge of good and evil you shall not eat, for in the day that you eat of it you shall surely die.
Genesis 2:16b–17, NKJV

God had already given man authority over all living creatures and responsibility before Eve arrived on the scene. Adam was operating in his purpose and Kingdom assignment. The Lord brought all the living creatures to Adam to see what he would call them; and whatever Adam called an animal, that was its name.

It was after this that the Lord placed Adam into a deep sleep and took one of his ribs in order to build the woman. Our God is awesome, and Adam had to be a large man for one rib to be used in order to build a woman! The wonderful revelation in this is that Adam knew exactly who Eve was when the Lord presented her to him. For he declared, "This creature is now bone of my bones and flesh of my flesh; she shall be called Woman, because she was taken out of man" (Genesis 2:23, AMPC).

Wouldn't it be wonderful if we all could have the initial experience that Adam and Eve had? Adam was given dominion and operated in sweat-less effort. Eve never had to wonder if she would be found and get married because her mate was there the moment she opened her eyes. Neither of them had to experience heartbreak and the rigors of dating to discover who their soulmate may be. So, why do singles today seemingly go through such toil and strain to realize the simple pleasures of marriage and companionship?

The root of all pain, heartache, disappointment, or confusion that we as people have experienced is connected to sin. This concept extends itself in application to singles. God had instructed Adam that he could freely eat of every tree of the garden; but that he must not eat of the tree of the knowledge of good and evil, for in the day that he does eat of that tree, he shall surely die. "For the wages of sin is death, but the gift of God is eternal life in Christ Jesus our Lord" (Romans 6:23, NKJV).

Understand that this death was not a sudden physical death, but that day, mankind began to die.

Man was made in the image and likeness of God and was not made to experience death. Adam lived to be 930 years old, but now the average human in the United States lives to be approximately 78.7 years old. The lifespan of humans has significantly shortened since the days of old.

Consider that in Adam's day, there were no gyms, no emergency rooms, nor were there prescription medications, yet he lived over 900 years. Everything that was necessary to sustain Adam, Eve, and all the animals was provided. Compare that to current day. Even with the technological advancements that have provided waves of hope for those battling disease, mankind has been unable to completely outsmart death. If Adam could have imagined the long-term effects of his decision to disobey God, I highly doubt that he would have taken that bite.

Have You Ever Asked Why?

Notice that Adam and Eve had everything at their disposal. They literally had it made! God had given them access to every beautiful tree imaginable and made sure that those trees would provide food to satisfy their pallet. However, it was man's desire for that which was forbidden that changed how the world would operate. It began as a thought and then became an action. One little seemingly harmless bite changed everything for humanity. Make a mental note of this point as it will be discussed more in depth later.

As a result of Adam's sin, mankind fell from Grace and provided a legal avenue for sin and calamity to enter the earth. Disobedience brought forth death, sickness, hard labor for men, and labor pains for women. Man was no longer in right standing with God. This is the underlying reason as to why bad things happen to good people some-times—because sin is in the earth. Sin and evil are the driving forces behind sickness, tragedy, murder, disappointments, and even heartbreak. Before the fall of man, everything was perfect.

In Genesis Chapter 4, Adam and Eve had two sons, Cain, a farmer, and Abel, a herdsman. One day they both brought an offering to God. Cain brought some produce from his farm and Abel brought choice cuts of meat. Abel received God's approval, but Cain did not and started pouting. Cain was then angry at Abel and subsequently killed his own brother simply because God rewarded him.

As you can see, tragedy and unfavorable circumstances started with the first family. The Lord instructed Cain that since he murdered his brother, that he would be a homeless wanderer. In observation of this passage,

> ## It began as a thought and then became an action.

we may be able to identify with Abel in that he was doing what he believed was right, yet he was harmed by someone close to him. Hence, God commands us to walk in love so that we are not given over to the spirit of hatred, jealousy, or rage.

We must not be like Cain, who joined the Evil One and then killed his brother. And why did he kill him? Because he was deep in the practice of evil, while the acts of his brother were righteous. So don't be surprised, friends, when the world hates you. This has been going on a long time.
I John 3:12–13, MSG

There are several examples in the Bible of good people experiencing tragedy because of evil in the hearts of others. Consider the story of King Saul and David in the Old Testament. After David had killed Goliath, the people began celebrating him. This made Saul jealous and he was then bent on killing David.

> When the victorious Israelite army was returning home
> after David had killed the Philistine, women from all the
> towns of Israel came out to meet King Saul. They sang
> and danced for joy with tambourines and cymbals. This
> was their song: "Saul has killed his thousands, and David
> his ten thousands!" This made Saul very angry.
> I Samuel 18:6–8a, NLT

Saul allowed his insecurities to get the best of him. Soon thereafter, he flung a spear at David in an attempt to pin him to the wall. Fortunately, David escaped but he would spend the next several years watching his back because of Saul's temper tantrums. Nonetheless, David maintained his integrity and did not kill Saul when he had the opportunity. David assured Saul that he had no intentions on rendering evil for evil because his heart was pure. He told Saul, "From evil people come evil deeds" (I Samuel 24:13a, NLT). Based on the facts, Saul could have easily been charged and convicted of several counts of attempted murder, and David could have justifiably retaliated in self-defense. But, since David did not have evil in his heart, he did not desire to take Saul's life. David would eventually become king and go down in history as a man after God's own heart.

There are other accounts of those that had hardships, financial problems, and diseases and the Lord provided the answer to their dilem-mas. Job is a classic example. While there are many lessons to be learned within the Book of Job, for the purposes of this training, we will focus on the issue of why the righteous may suffer. Job was considered a perfect and upright man. Recall that Job was very wealthy and had a beautiful family, yet he would experience some knockouts while in the ring with tragedy.

> There was a man in the country of Uz named Job. He was a man
> of perfect integrity who feared God and turned away from evil.
> One day the sons of God[6] came to present themselves before the
> Lord, and Satan also came with them. The Lord asked Satan,
> "Where have you come from?" "From roaming through the
> earth," Satan answered him, "and walking around on it."
> **Job 1:1, 6–7, HCSB**

Now, notice that during the conversation, Satan told God that he was walking around on the earth. Satan was once an angel, Lucifer. He was created in perfect beauty and music permeated from his very being! But then he became lifted in pride and wanted to exalt his throne above the throne of Almighty God. Epic fail.

Once Lucifer allowed his beauty to go to his head, God kicked him out of heaven, and he crashed onto the earth. See, Ezekiel 28:14–17. This explains how he got to earth and eventually gained access to Eve in the Garden of Eden in order to raise doubts in her mind about God's instructions concerning the forbidden tree. So, since Satan was kicked out of heaven and was roaming the earth, he decided to take his frustra-tions out on everyone else, which included God's servant, Job.

In Job 1:8, God asked Satan if he had considered Job. God agreed to remove the hedge of safety from Job, but that Satan could not take his life. At that point, Job experienced sickness, loss of loved ones, and he lost all his material possessions. Each believer should recognize that we have God's protection from unfortunate circumstances and Satan cannot touch us unless God allows him to. If God permits it, then it will be for His glorious purpose. [7] Job continued to love God throughout his test and reached a new level of humility and faith. In the end, God blessed him with twice what he had before.

Maybe you can identify with Job. Perhaps you have lost loved ones and have wondered why. Know that God allows certain things to happen in our lives, not to hurt us, but to develop His character in us and to bring glory to His throne.

In John 9, Jesus saw a man who was blind from birth. The disciples asked Him, "Who sinned, this man or his parents that he was born blind?" Jesus answered and said, "Neither this man nor his parents sinned, but this happened so that the works of God might be displayed in him" (NIV). If you believe that you have undergone some things in life that seem unfair, then know that you are not alone. Remember that God will always be glorified even in tribulation.

> **The root of all pain, heartache, disappointment, or confusion that we as people have experienced is connected to sin.**

You may find other examples in Scripture or in history that resemble your life's story. The Book of Ruth is powerful in that it provides the connecting link in the lineage of the Lord Jesus. We established that Christ has defeated sin and all forces of evil on the cross. But then again, there had to be a means by which He would arrive on earth through the human race so that the Scriptures would be fulfilled.

In studying the Book of Ruth, you will see that Naomi, her husband Elimelech, and their two sons left Bethlehem because of a famine and lived in Moab for a while. Eventually, Elimelech died and Naomi remained in Moab as a widow. Her sons married Moabite women, Orpah and Ruth. Naomi's two sons eventually died, and she was left without her husband and her children. At this point, Naomi and her daughters-in-law, Orpah and Ruth, are all widows. Can you imagine the magnitude of heartbreak that they all felt? Naomi decided to return home to Bethlehem and Ruth accompanied her.

During that time, kinsmen or family redeemers were relatives who would buy back family members from debt or redeem land.[7] Since Boaz was Elimelech's relative, he was a family redeemer and was willing to essentially buy back Naomi's property. Along with that, he would marry Ruth and perpetuate the names of Elimelech and Mahlon, Ruth's deceased husband.

Although Ruth had not had a child previously, she and Boaz would give birth to Obed, the father of Jesse, and grandfather of David. Once again, God was glorified in the midst of tragedy. Even though Ruth and Naomi suffered loss, they had pivotal roles in history and are a part of the lineage of our King, not to mention they both became wealthy once Boaz married Ruth!

I find my story connected to the woman with the issue of blood. In Luke Chapter 8, you will see that the woman suffered from hemorrhaging for 12 years, spending all of her money on doctors to no avail. As a teenager, I had difficulties in this area and the problem continued into adulthood.

The Scripture does not indicate why this happened to this particular woman. Perhaps it was genetics. I am certain that she wondered why she was stricken with such a condition. I wondered the same thing: "Why?" Perhaps God and Satan had a conversation about her just as they did regarding Job.

The good news is that even though Satan was given access to the world, subjecting humanity to sickness, disease, and hardship, God was not caught by surprise. The shedding of Jesus's blood took care of it all. Thankfully, I realized that since the woman with the issue of blood was healed as a result of her belief, that I have access to the same privilege.

I began to believe God for divine healing and in the midst of doing so, He directed my path to some excellent doctors that knew exactly how to resolve my issue! God is my healer, but He used earthly doctors as instruments. I am continuing to stand in faith and proclaim divine health.

All Things Work Together For Good

Satan seeks to run interference in people's lives in different ways. Today, there are men and women who have never witnessed the Godly examples of what it means to be Kingdom husbands and wives. There are generational and family issues, such as divorce, childbirth out of wedlock and same sex attractions that plague our communities. Furthermore, there are hurting singles left to believe that God is not concerned about their happiness and subsequently turn to temporary antidotes to fix long-term issues.

While the aforementioned examples of hardship vary in nature, they all have similar effects and can cause individuals to be discouraged and feel forsaken. Whether we experience perplexing times because of physical, emotional, or financial difficulties, we can always rely on the power of the Holy Spirit to strengthen us.

Perhaps, if we never experience challenges or heartbreak, we would not tap into the comforting and healing power of the Holy Spirit. Jesus set the ultimate example because he was despised and rejected, yet He was without sin. If He came out on top, so will we!

And we know that all things work together for good to those who love God, to those who are the called according to His purpose.
Romans 8:28, NKJV

We must maintain the attitude that Joseph had in the Book of Genesis. His brothers hated him, sold him into slavery, and convinced their father that he had been eaten by a wild animal. While in slavery in Egypt, Joseph endured accusations of coming on to his master's wife and was thrust into prison.

Ultimately, Joseph's gifts would make room for him and he would be promoted as an Egyptian ruler under Pharaoh's authority. When the worldwide famine finally came, Jacob, Joseph's father, sent 10 of his sons to Egypt for food. At the end of the story, Joseph revealed his identity to his family and was delighted that he was in a position to save their lives.

Joseph said to them, "Do not be afraid, for am I in the place of God? But as for you, you meant evil against me; but God meant it for good, in order to bring it about as it is this day, to save many people alive."
Genesis 50:19–20, NKJV

What a noble man Joseph was! He could have abused his authority and made his brothers pay for selling him into slavery. However, he knew that God placed him in a position of power to be an instrument in saving the lives of his family members. As singles, we can study the Word of God and find countless instances in which individuals may have experienced grief, yet God was with them. This is what you should gather from the scriptural examples. Thanks be to God! He did not leave us hanging as a result of Adam and Eve's sin. He had the ultimate plan in place.

As referenced on Training Day 1, Jesus came to redeem mankind and gave us access to healing, wholeness, prosperity, and everlasting life. Because of His redeeming power, we can overcome heartbreak and fulfill our purpose and assignments that He preordained for us. There is no issue that we may face that cannot be covered under the blood of Jesus.

> For we are God's [own] handiwork (His workmanship), recreated in
> Christ Jesus, [born anew] that we may do those good works which
> God predestined (planned beforehand) for us [taking paths which
> he prepared ahead of time], that we should walk in them [living
> the good life which he prearranged and made ready for us to live].
> **Ephesians 2:10, AMPC**

Simply put, God created you to do amazing things! We are God's masterpieces. Each of us has a special path that God has already walked out before us. It is up to us to receive His Grace, which is His divine enablement, to carry out the work that He has given us to do. Now is the time for you to break free from your paralysis caused by heartache, failures, or doubt.

Like God freely gave Adam dominion over the earth and gave him instructions to tend to the Garden of Eden, we have been given all things through Christ's redemptive work. Our job may not be to tend to the

> **If God permits it, then it will be for His glorious purpose.**

Garden of Eden, but we do have the responsibility to guard our hearts, for out of it springs the issues of life. Christ has defeated heartbreak, and we must tend to our gardens, our hearts. (Proverbs 4:23, NKJV).

We are not responsible for what other people do to us and some things happen that are beyond our control. On the other hand, we are responsible for how we respond to people and circumstances, and we must ensure that we do not allow bitterness to settle in our hearts. Even if we have caused pain for someone else, we do not have to receive condemnation because we are forgiven and cleansed through His blood. We should still seek to use wisdom and ask others for forgiveness if we have wronged them.

It is imperative that you receive the healing that Christ has provided in this single season and take the necessary steps to overcome condemnation, heartbreak, and disappointment. These negative thoughts and emotions cloud our ability to be effective in life, ministry, and in communion with God. I have personally experienced emotional trauma that caused me to nearly check out on my purpose in life, the details of which will be discussed later. Thankfully, I was able to overcome!

Your heart should be comforted in knowing that some things that have happened to you or circumstances that have affected you are not always a result of some sin that you committed. Some things happen because of sin in the earth or trials that test our faith. Whatever the reason for your situation, God is worthy of praise because He will provide a way of escape so that we are able to bear any temptation or trial. As a result, you should be growing stronger every SINGLE moment you think of His goodness!

ROUND 1

Congratulations! You've survived the warm-up. Let's move on to the next phase of training.

Training Day 3

Get Naked

Now that you have an appreciation for the victory that Christ has provided for us, we can delve into the action plan for overcoming heartbreak. Then, you can experience the manifestation of emotional healing. The initial critical step on the road to wholeness is to "get naked." In order to tap into true freedom and wholeness, which lends itself to true mental, emotional and spiritual health, we must be willing to become vulnerable before God concerning issues in our lives and areas in our hearts.

Some of our struggles may involve the following: 1) issues that we have not gotten over, 2) issues we are angry about, 3) issues we feel are unfair, 4) issues we are embarrassed about, or 5) issues we do not want to discuss because of shame, pain, unforgiveness, or resentment. These are the crime scene areas that are taped off so that no one can go beyond them, including the Lord. Many times, we may have experienced hardships or life-altering situations and then resorted to using the "out of sight, out of mind" coping mechanism to convince ourselves that we are OK. I'm guilty. This is a ploy of pride and deception that prevents total freedom. It is OK to not be OK!

Remember that being in a relationship or being married does not equate to being healed or happy. There are many dysfunctional homes and relationships because someone decided to mask his or her pain instead of acknowledging it. Two broken people can be together and make their relationship work, but is the relationship fruitful or stressful? Will either party live up to his or her full potential? Is God being glorified in the relationship?

When we are broken, we have a tendency to attract other broken people. In doing this can risk the possibility of never walking in our God-given purpose or fulfilling our destiny. We must seek God for healing instead of seeking healing in individuals and romantic companionship. When we look to be made whole by another person that may also be seeking to fill a void, we are setting ourselves up for disappointment.

Two hurting people can love each other; even so, they may place an undue burden on one another to meet needs that only God can meet. For example, if a person has been in a relationship in which his or her significant other or spouse was unfaithful, then he or she may struggle with trust as a result. If that person does not allow God to mend the heart, then he or she will likely place an undue burden of perfection upon the subsequent partner as a result of past hurts.

It is difficult for two broken people to minister to the needs of each other. Many times, neither of them is equipped to meet the needs of the other as they believe. That is why it is important to heal after failed relationships. If not, we will seek to satisfy the itch that the last individual did

> **When we are broken, we have a tendency to attract other broken people.**

38

not scratch with someone new who may not be assigned to our lives in any capacity other than a friend or an associate. These types of emotional decisions may cause us to place ourselves in positions of compromise.

Relationships are about more than chemistry, cuddling, goosebumps, and good looks. They involve the intertwining of purpose, spirits and souls, especially when sex is involved. Sexual contact should not be a part of any non-marital relationship and there are reasons why. Of course, we must consider what the Word of God says concerning the matter.

> *Therefore, a man shall leave his father and*
> *mother and shall become united and cleave to*
> *his wife, and they shall become one flesh.*
> **Genesis 2:24, AMPC**

Notice that the scripture states that the two shall become one flesh. This indicates that God's original intention was that when a man and woman join together as husband and wife, they should not separate. In addition to their sexual union, they would come together in emotional, mental, and spiritual harmony.[8]

The sexual act is the consummation, or completion, of marriage. Sex is designed for procreation, but it is also an instrument used to bring oneness to marriage. Have you ever wondered why it was difficult to get beyond certain people after a breakup? Or, have you wondered why you picked up another person's habits or personality? If sexual activity has taken place, then a soul tie has been created. Our souls should only be tied to the Lord and to the one we have joined in Holy matrimony.

Don't you know that your bodies are a part of Christ's body?
So should I take a part of Christ's body and make it part of a
prostitute? Absolutely not! Don't you know that anyone joined
to a prostitute is one with her? For Scripture says, the two shall
become one flesh. But anyone joined to the Lord is one with
Him. Run from sexual immorality! Every sin that a person
can commit is outside the body. On the contrary, the person
who is sexually immoral sins against his own body. Don't you
know that your body is a sanctuary of the Holy Spirit who is in
you, whom you have from God? You are not your own, for you
were bought with a price. Therefore glorify God in your body.
I Corinthians 6:16–20, HCSB

Here, Paul instructed the church at Corinth to flee fornication, which
is sex outside of the confines of marriage. Any time that we partake in
sexual activity with a person, we are becoming one with that person,
even if the person is a prostitute! Paul states that we are a part of Christ's
body and we should not join our bodies to anyone else in unholy sexual
behavior. Our duty is to glorify God with our bodies by abstaining.

It is God's will that you should be sanctified: that you should
avoid sexual immorality; that each of you should learn to
control your own body in a way that is holy and honorable, not
in passionate lust like the pagans who do not know God.
I Thessalonians 4:3–5, NIV

The goal of this training day is to encourage you to "get naked," but
only in a spiritual and emotional sense in relation to the Father. It is

clear what God's instructions are concerning sexual purity. If we truly desire to please Him, we will not seek to find ways to bend or adjust the standard of holiness in order to satisfy our desires. We will discuss this topic in more depth on Training Day 9, but let these passages resonate with you for now.

If you have stepped outside of the bounds of marriage and have engaged in such unholy behavior, then do not beat yourself up. Just repent so that God can restore you spiritually. Furthermore, you want to pray so that God will rid you of any ungodly soul ties. Pray this prayer of restoration: "Father, I denounce and cancel all soul ties and spiritual connections that are not of you by the blood of Jesus. I repent for going against your plan for my life. Cleanse me with your Holy Spirit. I receive your righteousness. Amen."

Once you've prayed that prayer, then you are cleansed and forgiven. Do not allow the enemy to bring condemnation upon you. Our God is faithful and just to forgive us and He throws our sins into the sea of

> **Just repent so that God can restore you spiritually.**

forgetfulness, never to remember them. Since He is faithful and just to forgive us, then we must learn to forgive ourselves.

In some of my dating experiences, I am guilty of leaving one relationship heartbroken and then subsequently entering a relationship with someone new because he had qualities that were missing in the previous relationship. In hindsight, I realized that I was not sober when I entered the subsequent relationship. I was unable to readily identify the obvious dysfunction of the new relationship because I was blinded by some of the present desired qualities that were absent from the previous situation. For that reason, I conceded to the dysfunction and unhappiness because I convinced myself that the new situation was better than the old one.

These types of connections are based upon the filling of voids and NOT Kingdom purpose. What happens when the temporary or superficial need is no longer there? The relationship becomes obsolete and we end up carrying dead weight because of a refusal to let go. We must be willing to show God all our cards. Lay everything on the table so that He can heal every inch of our hearts. Those with children must be careful not to neglect your own mental health and emotional healing by pouring all your energy into the children. You cannot be your greatest asset to them while continuously putting Band-Aides on wounds. I understand that sometimes when we experience unfavorable events, it is easy to realign our energy and bury ourselves into external sources in order to cope with losses.

I do not have children, but I do have a niece, nephews, other family members and friends. Additionally, I have a very strenuous work schedule at times. While it is perfectly normal to adjust our daily routines when a loved one or significant other is no longer a part of our lives, we must ensure that we are not using our family, friends, children, or careers as temporary antidotes, or steroid shots.

Notice that in some cases, steroid shots only camouflage or numb the symptoms rather than resolving the underlying issues. This is equivalent to placing Band-Aides on gunshot wounds. If a person does not properly tend to the injury and continues to attempt to live life normally, pretending that the big hole of exposed flesh is not there, he will eventually bleed to death.

Instead of burying yourself into other things and people as a form of denial, I implore you to deal with your hurts. Dealing with it may include counseling, more devotional periods, journaling, a vacation alone, or just decompression time. You will appreciate yourself for taking this time, and so will those that need you.

Vulnerability, Transparency, and Trust

In order to get to a place of total restoration, we must learn to pull the guards down. True vulnerability requires transparency. We may struggle with transparency with people, but we must get to a place of total nakedness and vulnerability with God. This requires faith and total trust.

If we are honest, sometimes we tend to trust God more in one area than another. For instance, we may trust Him to provide a job, but not the right mate. Some may also have a hard time believing that He will provide financially. We must allow ourselves to be completely vulnerable with the King in order that we may fully develop our trust in Him. Psalm 138:8a says, "The Lord will perfect that which concerns me" (AMPC). God is the ultimate problem solver, but we must be willing to take down our guards and give Him full access.

Any object, endeavor, or person that becomes more important than God's will and purpose for our lives is an idol. Our pride, feelings, emotions, and even our agenda can become an idol. That is why it is imperative that we remain humble before God with a willingness to show Him every puncture and scar of our hearts.

Years ago, I went through a heart wrenching break-up. I thought that we would eventually marry (even though there was a lot of dysfunction). When that relationship ended, I was devastated. I could not concentrate and I could not operate in ministry as effectively as I should have. I was not sinking myself into purpose; I was sinking myself into pity, depression, shame, and bad habits. It was not until I became vulnerable before God that I was able to start picking up the pieces and moving toward wholeness.

The key to my vulnerability with the Lord included extended quiet time in prayer, worship, meditation, and in seeking wise counsel. In those moments, I was able to commune with God and allow the guards to fall. Before then, I allowed myself to be distracted and busy so that I would not have to face my own painful truth, which was that I was hurt, sad, angry, and even a little perturbed at God because things didn't pan out the way I thought they should. I also discovered that I had a little pride in my heart because I told God, "I am Jessica Yarbrough and I should be married by now!"

> **True vulnerability requires transparency.**

When I became naked before God and stopped being angry, then God was able to speak to me. He said, "You are hurt because the relationship did not work out, yes. But you are more hurt because you were more fixated on the idea of what YOU thought should be. YOU BEGAN TO IDOLIZE YOUR OWN AGENDA!" Ouch. Not only had I made my agenda more important than my purpose, I was trying to make God's agenda fit what I had in mind and on my timetable.

During some past relationships, I struggled with happiness. As a matter of fact, while in one relationship, God told me: "Find happiness elsewhere and you will be indifferent as to whether this relationship works out or not." He did this in order to help spare my emotions and mental stability once the relationship ended because He knew that we would go our separate ways. Unfortunately, I did not take heed and almost went over the deep end. Depression, anxiety, and negative thoughts were ever present. It was difficult to let go of many of my past relationships. One reason was because of my loyalty and love. I do not fall in love quickly, but when I do, I land hard. Another reason was because of fear. Fear of being alone, starting over again, and meeting someone new. However, fear should never be the driving force behind our decisions, and especially not relationships. Fear is not of God.

Becoming naked and transparent before anyone can be very uncomfortable. Despite that, it is a beautiful experience when we take off our outer garments before God and allow Him to inspect us. Doing so allows us to be honest with ourselves because He already knows the details of what we are so desperately trying to hide. It also helps us to surrender to His healing power.

There are some people who hate going to the doctor. Sometimes, the doctor's visit calls for unclothing and putting on the thin medical gown. Some of the gowns are open in the front and some have a string to tie in the back. Either way, they are designed so that the nurse or physician has easy access to our bodies for inspection or surgery. Regardless of how ashamed or uncomfortable we are, we realize that our ultimate goal is to receive the necessary medical treatment that will be beneficial to us in the end. Therefore, we suck it up and get naked because the benefit of the treatment will greatly outweigh the discomfort or shame.

Imagine a heart failure patient griping about having to get into a skimpy gown when her life is on the line. Doesn't that sound crazy? We would all admonish her to forget about the gown and just get the help. If we can strip down at the doctor's office or at the hospital, then certainly we can "get naked" in front of God.

It is an amazing feeling when we can accept that God is not out to hurt us. He only wants to help us and desires to see us live our best lives. But, in order to get to the desired destination of wholeness, we must take the proper steps that begin with transparency with the Father. Thus, I'm challenging you to begin removing those outer garments of fear, unforgiveness, sadness, loneliness, or whatever may be keeping you from being vulnerable at the feet of Jesus. Don't allow pride and the fear of discomfort to kill you. Get help. Get treated.

As a matter of fact, mankind's original state was a naked one. Adam and Eve were naked and unashamed. "And they were both naked, the man and his wife, and were not ashamed" (Genesis 2:25, NKJV). While they were not clothed in physical garments, I believe that they were clothed with the Glory of God.

As a result of Adam's sin, he and Eve became ashamed before God of their nakedness and covered themselves. They had fallen from God's Glory and their sins had separated them from fellowship with our Father. Now, not only were they physically naked, but they had become spiritually, emotionally, and relationally naked. Notice that Adam and Eve were naked from the start, but after they sinned, they became exposed and vulnerable.

God did not change; Adam and Eve did. God loved them in their nakedness, but they became uncomfortable with it. A barrier was placed between God and man. That is why we have moments of hurt, shame, and discomfort today. We may feel ashamed or uncomfortable before God because of issues in our heart, but God already sees us just as we are. He knows what concerns us and He is the one who can address all our problems. Nothing catches God by surprise. Remember that Jesus has restored mankind back to our rightful place with God. We are no longer

condemned and do not have to
be ashamed in our nakedness
before Him. The act of removing
our outer garments will bring
us closer to our humble identity that God intended for us to
have: an identity of righteous-

> **It also helps us to surrender to His healing power.**

ness that is clothed with the presence and Glory of Almighty God.

My charge to you is to "get naked" if you haven't already. Do not try
to camouflage your emotional, spiritual, or mental vulnerability by cov-
ering it with superficial security. Examples of superficial security include
prematurely beginning a new relationship or denying that counseling
and healing is needed.

Another example of false security is attempting to appear overly spiritual and religious instead of dealing with internal issues. Some issues
cannot be shouted over but must be dealt with in prayer and with wise
counsel. If various forms of superficial security have been your mode of
operation, then I pray that this book will inspire you to take a different route. God can see through the projected images anyway. He is just
waiting on you to acknowledge your symptoms so that He can address
the real problems and provide you with abundant healing. It is OK to
be comfortable being alone for a while. It is possible to be alone without
being lonely.

I encourage you to pour your heart out to God, whether in prayer,
in song, or by writing a letter. Tell Him exactly how you feel and leave
no stone unturned because He is the great physician! He specializes in
every area known to man. He created us in His image and likeness. As
a result, He knows how many hairs are on our heads and how many

ounces of blood are running through our veins. He also knows all about our struggles and disappointments.

It is comforting to know that our Father created us and cares for us, so we do not have to be ashamed of revealing our innermost secrets and concerns to Him. Hand your broken heart to Him. This is a critical step on the road to healing and fulfillment.

Training Day 4

Beware of Disappointments

By now you should be feeling lighter after having released the weight of all the burdens that you've been carrying. We were not made to carry burdens; it is our responsibility to cast our cares upon Him. The goal is to receive strength after thrusting our heartaches and concerns upon the Lord.

> Casting all your care upon Him, for He cares for you. Be sober, be vigilant; because your adversary the devil walks around like a roaring lion, seeking whom he may devour. But may the God of all grace, who called us to His eternal glory by Christ Jesus, after you have suffered a while, perfect, establish, strengthen, and settle you.
> **I Peter 5:7–8, 10, NKJV**

It is necessary that we allow ourselves to become transparent with God concerning the vicissitudes of life that plague us as singles. On the other hand, we must not worship those moments or build monuments around our disappointments. This Kingdom strategy is applicable to every area of our lives. Relishing in the thoughts and feelings of what happened to us will create a vicious cycle of defeat and delay our healing.

Disappointments are not uncommon, but they will grow into discouragement if unattended. Discouragement, when left not combatted, can lead to a total loss of hope and confidence. This is one of Satan's tactics to devour us. Since Jesus has already defeated Satan, if we are not sober, Satan will cause us to wallow in negative thoughts so that we do not walk in the victory that is rightfully ours.

Some of these negative thoughts are self-inflicted distractions. I must warn you that after you have stripped to nakedness before the King, do not allow the spirit of disappointment to linger. We begin idolizing and praising our hurt when we magnify it above God, His Sovereignty and Grace, and what He is able to do. Amplifying our pain above the Problem Solver causes us to remain stuck and to not receive the manifestation of the emotional, spiritual, and mental healing that we so desperately need.

Remember that the Lord came to heal the brokenhearted, not to provide ice cream and cake at pity parties for hearts to remain shattered. Once we go to God unclothed and vulnerable, we must then ignite worship and praise, thanking Him for His power and His love for us. Recall what we discussed about Prophet Isaiah's foreshadowing in the Old Testament of the coming Messiah and the victory that He would provide for those that receive Him:

The Spirit of the Lord is upon Me, Because the Lord has anointed Me to preach good tidings to the poor; He has sent Me to heal the brokenhearted, to proclaim liberty to the captives, And the opening of the prison to those who are bound; to proclaim the

acceptable year of the Lord, and the day of vengeance of our
God; to comfort all who mourn, to console those who mourn in
Zion, to give them beauty for ashes, the oil of joy for mourning,
the garment of praise for the spirit of heaviness…Instead
of your shame you shall have double honor; and instead of
confusion they shall rejoice in their portion. Therefore, in their
land they shall possess double; everlasting joy shall be theirs.
Isaiah 61:1–3, 7, NKJV

We can rejoice in that God is ready to make an uneven exchange with us and give us beauty for our ashes, the oil of joy for sadness, and He will bless us with double. If you are like me, you may have had countless disappointments in life. I have experienced let downs in career moves, friendships, and in relationships. Because of these events, I became weary, felt alone, and was suffering from emotional paralysis. I was temporarily unable to move forward with ministry because of disappointments.

> **If you are like me, you may have had countless disappointments in life.**

We cannot effectively sink ourselves into purpose if we are magnifying what we deem as the short end of the stick. Nevertheless, we do not realize how strong we are until faced with daunting challenges that should seemingly cause us to check out on life. Thankfully, God promised that He would not put more on us than we can bear. Our definition of "what we can bear" is often different from His. Still, He is merciful toward us even when we bring heartache upon ourselves.

51

Disappointment and its Effects

Disappointment can provide meaningful lessons that we can employ for future situations, but it is up to us to ensure that we do not fall prey to those disappointing circumstances. Disappointments, when allowed to linger, can lead us down dangerously dark paths that we would not have anticipated, full of depression or bitterness. It is during this time that bad habits can be developed, such as drug addictions, excessive drinking, promiscuity, or other superficially satisfying past times. Disappointments can cause individuals to begin behaving out of character. If such behavior continues, then over a period of time, the disappointing circumstance becomes obsolete, and the behavior that developed as a result becomes the norm.

The ultimate outcome of the repeated negative behavior is a change in one's character that is not representative of who the individual truly is. This is typically a coping mechanism or a concoction that makes matters worse. Satan's goal is not for us to only step out of character, but for us to remain out of character and to never live up to who God called us to be.

We must beware of who we entertain while in the valley of disappointment. In these times, we are not the best version of ourselves and are more susceptible to compromise. We may develop attachments with people based on emotional neediness. It is in these moments that we may concede that having somebody is better than having nobody. In my moments of despair, I came across some nice and intelligent people, but I realized that these individuals would not have had the capacity to receive me as I would have been if I was operating as the normal version of myself, without certain levels of compromise.

During these times of overwhelming disappointment, I was not as prayerful as I should have been, and I was not effectively focused on

Kingdom. I had lost spiritual discipline. I began behaving loosely and developing poor habits. So, I began to ask myself, "Do I like the person that I am becoming?" I did not. I was not operating as the righteous person that God made me. (The moment that we accept Christ into our lives, we take on our new identity in Him and our sins are washed away. We then receive Grace to walk in our new identity.) Some of the company that I was keeping did not check my behavior but welcomed it.

The connections that I had made helped to create environments that were conducive to compromise. I was in a sunken place and did not even know it. Eventually, I pondered that if my company is encouraging or allowing this behavior from me rather than helping to hold me accountable, where would I end up if these connections continue?

This is not to say that our friends or soulmates will not be flawed because we all are. Still, I knew that my life was out of alignment with God and the fruit which my life was bearing was not the real me. My behavior was a byproduct of disappointment. Consequently, I needed to readjust my mindset and move beyond that temporary stage of negative behavior so that I could ensure to live according to God's Word and attract positive connections that can accommodate where God is taking me.

Use Your Weapons

We cannot control all the elements in the environment, neither can we control what other people do. But we can control our own thoughts and actions through the power of the Holy Spirit. We have supernatural weapons at our disposal. Our spiritual weapons include prayer, praise, worship and the Word of God.

*Since the weapons of our warfare are not worldly but are powerful
through God for the demolition of strongholds. We demolish
arguments and every high-minded thing that is raised up against
the knowledge of God, taking every thought captive to obey Christ.*
II Corinthians 10:4–5, HCSB

God has equipped us with the Kingdom tools necessary to over-throw and thwart the enemy's plans to bring us down. We are able to pray, fast, and speak the Word of God over our situations. However, we must have the faith to believe that we are victorious.

The comforting fact is that we are always able to rest in Christ's love for us, even amid crushing times. This mindset helps us to overcome the "why me" mentality in that we begin to understand that God's plan for our lives is far greater than our mistakes or any strategic plan that we could develop on our own.

Continual prayer and communion with God give us access to peace of mind. Along with prayer, it may be advantageous to seek professional counseling or medications for a period of time to help with the depression, insomnia, or anxieties that may have resulted from any traumatic experience, not just ones involving failed relationships. Developing a healthy diet and workout regimen will also help to relieve stress.[9]

Some Christians do not believe in seeking out professional counseling or taking prescribed mental health medications for various reasons. One must be persuaded in his or her own mind as to whether this is a viable or suitable option to assist on the road to recovery. Yes, we are overcomers of every circumstance, illness, or disease through the blood of Jesus. Then again, if one's faith is not yet perfected and effective in manifesting the physical, emotional, or mental healing that is needed, then perhaps therapy and medications can provide temporary assistance until one's faith is increased and healing manifests.

Dr. Sigmund Freud (1856–1939) was a renowned neurologist who studied physiology (how the body works) and neurology (how the brain works). Freud believed that we have conscious and unconscious parts of our minds and sought to help people with mental illness through psychoanalysis.[10] Psychoanalysis is the means by which Freud sought to assist his patients by helping them to remember their fears and pain that may have been suppressed or locked away in their unconscious mind. The more the patients talked, the more they would reveal about themselves and their history.[11]

Scientists today refer to Freud's work in addressing mental illnesses. Jaak Panksepp combined psychoanalytic thinking and neuroscience in order to derive at the theory of emotional systems.[12] According to Panksepp, there is a correlation between emotional systems and neuronal systems in the brain.

The seven emotional systems are: Seeking (exploration and learning), Rage, Fear, Lust, Care, Panic/Grief, and Play. Each of the individual emotional systems can be detected chemically in different locations in the brain and can become the dominant principle of the mind.[13] Note that a person's behavior will coincide with what is going on neurologically.

The Panic/Grief system provides the basis of attachment. Consequently, it is activated upon separation. The body has its own pain control system that releases natural opioid compounds to create endorphins in the brain. Endorphins are natural hormones that our body releases to help us feel relaxed and happy. The body also creates endorphins during exercise and provides somewhat of a "natural high." According to the neuro-psychoanalytic model of depression, dysfunction is likely to occur when there is an excessive activation of the Panic/Grief system due to the loss of an object of attachment, whether through death or a breakup.[14]

I had been through multiple painful breakups and had also experienced disappointments in my career, which led to financial difficulties. Over the course of a few years, I dealt with bouts of depression that would come and go, but I did not realize what I was experiencing. Each day would be mundane, and I felt like a groundhog, waking up every day to go through the motions, only to repeat the same thing.

I finally reached a breaking point when, after a relationship had ended, I was unable to function with a sound mind. I was met with overwhelming emotions and uncontrolled crying at times. I had a loss of appetite and had difficulty sleeping at night, which led to challenges with staying alert and focused during the day. Although I was talking to God daily, going to church and praising God, I needed some practical and medical attention to help with my physical indicators.

Eventually, I sought professional counseling and shared my symptoms. I learned that I was experiencing the signs of depression and anxiety which were brought on by crisis. The temporary period of counseling sessions and prescribed medications did wonders for me and helped to treat the symptoms and effects that were brought on by traumatic experiences. Although I sought a natural recourse, I did not just dismiss my spiritual weapons. I continued to pray and seek God as I took the medications as prescribed and attended the counseling sessions. As referenced on Training Day 1, heartbreak happens, and its effects are scientifically similar to physical illnesses. Once I was able to get a handle on my mental and emotional state of being, then I was able to think more clearly and even have more meaningful communication with God.

If you or someone you know is experiencing life-altering, emotional challenges, then do not be ashamed to seek out professional help. That assistance is a safe tool on the road to wholeness that provides a means to cope with difficulties, while prayer, praise, worship, and the Word of God ensures that we are overcomers. Some people receive instantaneous deliverance from their issues, while others receive gradual deliverance. Taking advantage of some of the aforementioned practical tools does not make one person less spiritual than another who opts not to do so. Often times, those that criticize others for seeking mental health attention are taking medications for physical conditions. We all must believe God to bring us through.

Note that the professional tools that I shared with you should never replace our spiritual weapons. If utilized, they should only be used in tandem with our spiritual weapons. Likewise, those that take prescription medications for physical ailments should take their medications as prescribed while believing God for divine healing. The principles are the same.

I have also found that taking communion in the privacy of my home is an effective way to build my confidence in God and in His love for me. Communion, according to Scripture, represents that we acknowledge what Christ has done for us on the cross in that He took all sickness, disease, worry, failure, and sin upon Himself, having defeated all these things for us, wiping all our slates clean.

If you are connected to a local church, then perhaps there is an elder or a spiritually seasoned individual in your congregation who can offer you emotional support. Do not go through these trying times alone. God is with you, but He also has vessels here on earth to accompany you on this journey to wholeness. Be careful not to isolate yourself. If you are feeling alone, then ask God to send a confidant or someone that you can trust and confide in.

> Why are you down in the dumps, dear soul? Why are you
> crying the blues? "Fix my eyes on God-soon I'll be praising
> again. He puts a smile on my face. He's my God."
> **Psalm 42:11, MSG**

Do You Want to Be Made Well?

As discussed on Training Day 2, unfavorable things happen to good people sometimes. Nonetheless, we have the responsibility of overcoming each obstacle that is placed before us. Do you recall the story in the Book of John of the paralyzed man that lay at the pool of Bethesda? The scripture tells us that the man had been paralyzed for 38 years and that he would lie at the pool along with many other sick people.

At appointed times, an angel of the Lord would go down into the pool and stir the waters, causing it to bubble up. Whoever stepped into the water first would be healed. Well, this is what happened when Jesus saw the man lying there:

> When Jesus noticed him lying there [helpless], knowing that
> he had already been a long time in that condition, He said
> to him, "Do you want to become well?" The invalid answered,
> "Sir, I have nobody when the water is moving to put me
> into the pool; but while I am trying to come [into it] myself,
> somebody else steps down ahead of me." Jesus said to him,
> "Get up! Pick up your bed (sleeping pad) and walk!"
> **John 5:6–7, 9, AMP**

You would think that after no more than a few hours or days of lying at the pool that this man would have developed a plan to get into the water, even if it meant roll over and fall into it! He was waiting on someone else to pick up his pieces. He was waiting on perfect conditions and blamed others for his state of being.

Notice that when Jesus asked the man if he wanted to be well, that he immediately began talking about what others did not do for him. There is a possibility that he had been in this state so long that he lost the

> **I was in a sunken place and did not even know it.**

drive to even reach for his healing. Even if what this paralyzed man said concerning other people getting into the pool ahead of him was accurate, it still does not erase his responsibility to go after his own healing with every fiber of his being.

Consider what emotions this man experienced through the course of the years. Anger? Resentment? Disappointment? Sadness? Despair? Jealousy? Envy? Suicidal thoughts? He may have been on an emotional rollercoaster at times and his emotional imbalances could have been justified. In spite of that, none of those thoughts would help him get any closer to being made whole. It wasn't until he did something that he would not normally do that his wholeness came. He believed, then he got up.

Perhaps you are not physically paralyzed, but you are suffering from emotional, mental, and spiritual paralysis because of a gut-wrenching and heart-crushing experience. You may be like the man at the pool of Bethesda, wanting to be free, but as time passed, you have found that your motivation to reach for freedom has diminished. It may even seem as though other people have gotten the healing, happiness, or blessings that you so greatly desired and that you are still stuck. Declare that today, the negative thoughts of your painful past end and that you receive grace to accept what you cannot change. Receive peace of mind and let go of the haunting feelings of disappointment, discouragement, and despair.

If the Lord were to ask you today, "Do you want to be made well?" What would you say? I challenge you not to rehearse and dwell on what others may have done to you, or even what they failed to do. The Lord already knows. It is extremely difficult to effectively embrace what lies ahead while focusing on what was or what could have been. So, let me remind you that God wants to bring your life into the new and refreshing experiences that He has prepared especially for you!

> Forget about what's happened; don't keep going over old history. Be alert, be present. I'm about to do something brand new! It's bursting out. Don't you see it? There it is! I'm making a road through the desert, rivers in the badlands.
> **Isaiah 43:18–19, MSG**

The Lord has so many great and precious promises that He wants to bestow upon His children. He longs to grant your heart's desires and to see you happy. But you must be determined to not allow disappointment to cause you to miss your appointment with divine destiny.

Dr. Craig Banks, my apostle and senior pastor, would often say that disappointment's purpose is to cause us to miss our divine appointments. For that reason, you cannot afford to stay "dis-appointed." He would also tell me that disappointments cause us to go in a deficiency pattern because weaknesses have patterns. Satan looks to seize upon disappointments so that we lose our confidence, our faith, and then begin to open doors of weaknesses. Whatever our vices or weaknesses are, we may run the risk of reverting to them if disappointment is allowed to linger.

In my career, I have seen hundreds of people who were once drug addicts fall prey to their choice of drug after a traumatic experience, such as divorce, death of a loved one, or financial strain. It is in these times that we must remember that God's thoughts toward us are thoughts of peace, and not evil, and He wants to bring us to an expected outcome (Jeremiah 29:11).

Know that a disappointment, a failure, or a traumatic event is just a moment. A moment is not your life; it is just a moment. When we realize how great our God is and how wonderful His thoughts are toward us, we should be strengthened with might in our spirit, leading us to let go of past disappointments, and equipping us to handle any that may arise in the future. Yes, disappointing moments may come, but they do not have to linger and win.

ROUND 2

Still with me? Can you feel your muscles burning yet?
Good. Keep going!

Training Day 5

Stay Focused – Look Forward

My mother has always been a pillar of strength for me. She has the right words of encouragement at the most befitting moments. One day I was venting to her and sharing my frustrations about singleness and how it seemed that situations had been so unfair. Her words were, "You just stay focused and look forward." In other words, stay focused on God, what He is doing, and look ahead in anticipation of what will manifest on your behalf.

In this season of singleness, we must learn the significance of and develop in the power of effective focus. Many of us know how to focus, even if it is merely because we have spent so much time focusing on the wrong things and people. We all have had to employ some level of focus in our lives, whether for work, school, or for learning a new hobby or skill.

We must now channel that energy into focusing on the right things: Kingdom purpose and the promises of God. When we have this mindset, we will not become so easily distracted by those old familiar things and certain people will not capture our attention the way they used to. Some people and situations do not deserve our attention. This certain level of focus involves more than being busy so that we can label ourselves productive. It involves a heightened level of discernment in this season. We should be locked in to our assignment and sensitive to what God is saying to us. Our goal must be to hear Him ever so clearly, no matter how minute the message may seem to be.

Keep your eyes straight ahead; ignore all sideshow distractions
Proverbs 4:25, MSG

Another translation states:

Let your eyes look right on [with fixed purpose],
and let your gaze be straight before you
AMPC

Yielding to Distractions Prevents Kingdom Character

This mandate of focus is not a means to live in denial or act as if situations or circumstances did not occur or do not exist. The purpose is to develop a fortitude that solidifies a determination that we will not be governed by or live our lives based on unfavorable events or our longing for companionship. Satan uses the tactic of distraction to prevent us from progressing into Kingdom character.

Previously, we discussed dealing with past hurts and issues that keep us from receiving our healing. At some point, the enemy knows that he no longer has to inflict any harm upon us because we will inflict the harm upon ourselves when we are reminded of a hurtful situation. We may begin immediately reliving the pain of a previous experience.

Whatever that thing is that Satan knows nags us; he just uses it to his advantage without necessarily inflicting new pain. Or in the alternative, he causes us to have new occurrences that resemble the old ones in order to

> **Some people and situations do not deserve our attention.**

reignite the flames of old wounds. These events can lead to a stronghold, which is a fortress or a hold. Examples of strongholds may be addictions, fornication, depression, lying, stealing, or any repetitive cycle that seems to be unbreakable.

The concept of focus is very key, especially after we have mismanaged our time by sulking in our failures and mishaps. There is a difference between properly grieving versus sulking. The grieving process is healthy and necessary. It allows for mental and emotional cleansing, whereby we are able to accept the curve ball that life has thrown, and we then employ mechanisms to live our lives beyond the tragedy or challenging experience. Sulking is comprised of continual deliberate choices to remain mentally and emotionally oppressed, and a refusal to move forward when the path has been made clear to do so.

Please keep in mind, this point of focus is far from a resolve of being "busy." This concept is about intentional efforts to:

- Understand and adhere to Kingdom principles,

- Operate in Kingdom purpose, and

- Live in a new dimension of freedom, wholeness, and spiritual sensitivity to God's voice.

It is necessary to understand and adhere to Kingdom principles in order to develop in the character of God. The first principle is that of love. God is love and it is His command that we love one another. We cannot continue to operate with the same old mindsets of the past and expect to move forward in the promises of God.

For example, one way to combat distractions is to sincerely learn to pray for those who we believe have wronged us. "But I say to you, love your enemies, bless those who curse you, do good to those who hate you, and pray for those who spitefully use you and persecute you, that you may be sons of your Father in heaven" (Matthew 5:44–45a, NKJV). My pastor, Dr. Sheryl Banks, teaches us extensively on the importance of having a personal prayer life. Praying for others after we have spent quality time in personal prayer for ourselves allows us to maintain the heart of forgiveness.

Another vital Kingdom principle is that of faith, which is discussed in more detail on Training Day 6. In order to have effective faith, we must first be established in love. We cannot walk in true, God-designed love without walking in faith. Neither can we walk in faith without walking in love.[15] Faith works by love. In other words, faith works through God and because He is the epitome of love having given His only Son, we are able to believe. Love is the conduit, or the channel, through which our faith flows. Even if you have read it before, take the time to study I Corinthians 13, in which Apostle Paul teaches us the necessity of love.

> Though I speak with the tongues of men and of angels, but have not love, I have become sounding brass or a clanging cymbal. And though I have the gift of prophecy, and understand all mysteries and all knowledge, and though I have all faith, so that I could remove mountains, but have not love, I am nothing.
> **I Corinthians 13:1–2, NKJV**

The Kingdom principles of love and faith are crucial to our development as believers, and particularly, as Kingdom singles. These principles allow us to understand and adhere to other Kingdom principles, such as giving, sowing, and serving. In the New Testament, Jesus is a living paramount picture of what it means to give and to serve in that He came to serve mankind and give His life for us.

In order to effectually operate in our Kingdom purpose without merely being busy, we must be rooted and grounded in love and faith. The more we mature in the areas of love, faith, giving, and serving, the more effective we will be when operating in our purpose. We will have a more in-depth discussion about operating in Kingdom purpose on Training Day 7. It is critical to shut out distractions in order to fulfill our purpose in the earth; thus, we must stay focused and look forward.

When I began to regain my focus, I increased my prayer time and started to walk in more love and forgiveness. I also began to meditate on the Word of God so that my faith would increase and give me the strength to "look forward" to the promises of God

> **I increased my prayer time and started to walk in more love and forgiveness.**

being manifested. As a result, my heart's desire was to give more of myself to God and to the work of the ministry. While doing these things, I sensed that the layers of bondage were loosed, and I was walking in freedom from my past. Negative thoughts and emotions sprang up less and less. At that point, I discovered that, "this is what the road to wholeness (completeness) feels like."

Because of my focus on the Lord, I became more intrigued to

commune with Him and I could hear His voice more clearly. One afternoon I was at a coffee shop and had ordered the "Vanilla Cream Coffee of the Day." I went to the sweetening station to add just enough cream and sweetener to taste. On the counter was a trash bin for the used straws and sweetener packets. I recall that I had disposed of most of my trash but left one tiny piece of paper on the counter. Since I was hurrying back to work, I left the paper there and thought, "It's no big deal."

I darted for the door with my coffee, keys and phone in hand when I heard the Lord speak to me (in Apostle Banks' voice) saying, "That is not excellence. You left that piece of paper on the counter and there was no paper there when you got there." I wanted to respond in my own defense, but there was nothing I could say to help my own case. So, I did not argue.

I turned around and went back to put the tiny piece of paper in the trash and upon approaching the sweetening station, I noticed that I had left my umbrella lying there. My initial thought was, "Lord, why didn't you just tell me that I forgot my umbrella instead of telling me about the piece of paper that no one cares about?" It had stopped raining, so my mind was not on my umbrella when I was initially headed toward the door. But then, I quickly realized that God was teaching me a valuable lesson on hearing His voice and being sensitive to His commands. This would not have been possible if I had remained distracted by outside circumstances.

On another occasion I was eating alone on my lunch break when I noticed a single mom and her three children sitting nearby. I noticed that one of the children was talking and the Lord began to reveal to me that the child was very special to Him. The Lord shared with me that there was a great calling on the boy's life and that the mother should continue to pray for him and keep him active in church.

At first, I questioned whether I should tell the mother for fear of seeming weird, but I received a reassurance from the Holy Spirit. I then stopped questioning myself and realized that my ear to hear had increased because I had shut out the noise. I shared with the mother what the Lord had told me, and she was amazed. The mother then revealed that her son had disciplinary issues in school and behavioral issues at home, but that she was encouraged by what I had shared. She vowed to continue praying for her son and to keep him in a godly environment.

I was so glad that I was obedient because I did not want the blood to be on my hands. Being sensitive to God's voice and His commands can save your life or someone else's; hence, it is vital to adhere to the simplest of instructions from the Lord so that when the complicated directives come, following His lead will be second nature. It is dangerous to be distracted and lose your sense of awareness.

As singles, it is vital that we conquer the spirit of distraction and develop discipline instead of waiting until marriage to do so. It is unwise when individuals go into marriage without having developed the ability to divert and defeat distractions. They do not disappear upon saying "I do." Distractions are wrapped in deception and deceptions typically do not appear to be distractions at first glance. You will think that you are cognizant of all your surroundings, but you are not and will risk being blind-sided and ensnared.

Mark out a straight path for your feet; stay on the safe path.
Don't get sidetracked; keep your feet from following evil.
Proverbs 4:26–27, NLT

Is it an Idol?

I mentioned that after prior relationships, I was engulfed in sadness, depression, and anxiety. I could not get my mind off what happened when some of my significant others were unfaithful and how it made me feel. Subsequently, I began indulging in unhealthy behavior. I was entertaining too many people and too many different spirits. I had begun to let my guard down and become comfortable in the company of complete strangers just because they were handsome and were giving me the attention that I thought I wanted. I lost my focus. I challenge you to take the time for a self-assessment into what your thought life is like.

Ask yourself, "What consumes my thoughts? Are these thoughts helpful, harmful, or productive?" As singles, if we are constantly thinking about our longing for companionship, then there is a strong likelihood that we have become consumed, if not obsessed, with the desire for a romantic relationship. We must make certain that nothing consumes our thought life more than God and His Word.

While it is normal to think pleasant and wholesome thoughts of being happy and in love, we must be watchful that those thoughts do not become the driving force of our entire lives, goals, ambitions, and daily decisions. The key is to operate in balance. Pleasing God should be an utmost priority each day.

There are some good things that may come our way that are not designed to be distractions but have the tendency to develop into such when we begin to idolize them. It is a great thing to desire marriage, but we should not idolize the idea and desire for marriage so much that we become bitter when it does not happen on our timetable. When this happens, we look for substitutes to take the place of what God has ordained because we cannot hear the Lord's instructions over the outcries of our selfish wants. This concept is true for a myriad of areas in our lives in which we may have a strong want. It is dangerous to accept substitutes because of impatience.

My dad told me the story of how when he was a teenager, he wanted and needed a car. He told God, "Lord, I need a car." But apparently, he believed that the Lord was taking too long to make good on the deal, so my dad said he went and got a car without the Lord's help. Well, the car he picked out would not back up! Can you imagine having to always find a place to turn around? How inconvenient and embarrassing! Imagine being parked at Wal-Mart and someone is parked in front of you. You would have to wait until they finish shopping in order to leave so that you could drive forward. He was too focused on his need and what he wanted instead of focusing on God's promises and His instructions. God knows what we need and He also knows how and when to deliver it to us.

This type of behavior is nothing new. In the Book of Exodus, there is a story about how God used Moses to deliver the children of Israel out of slavery in Egypt. Later, Moses received instructions from the Lord that he passed along to the Israelites about how they should conduct themselves. Then, God had Moses to go up Mount Sinai so that He could give Moses more specific instructions and that is also where God gave him the inscribed 10 Commandments.

Moses was on the mountain for 40 days and nights and the Israelites grew tired of waiting.

> **I challenge you to take the time for a self-assessment into what your thought life is like.**

Instead of waiting patiently, they became idle and distracted, failing to adhere to the instructions that Moses had given them prior to his departure to Mount Sinai. They wanted a god that they could see, so they made their own idols.

> When the people realized that Moses was taking forever in coming down off the mountain, they rallied around Aaron and said, "Do something. Make gods for us who will lead us. That Moses, the man who got us out of Egypt—who knows what's happened to him?" So, Aaron told them, "Take off the gold rings from the ears of your wives and sons and daughters and bring them to me." They all did it; they removed the gold rings from their ears and brought them to Aaron. He took the gold from their hands and cast it in the form of a calf, shaping it with an engraving tool. The people responded with enthusiasm: "These are your gods, O Israel, who brought you up from Egypt!"
> **Exodus 32: 1–8, MSG**

The children of Israel lost their focus and allowed themselves to be distracted. They began operating in total disobedience and lost their sensitivity to God's voice even after they had been delivered from oppression in Egypt. They were so consumed by their desires for a visible ruler, that they created their own substitute god in the form of a molten calf. This greatly displeased God.

Romans 12:2 states, "And do not be conformed to this world, but be transformed by the renewing of your mind, that you may prove what is that good and acceptable and perfect will of God" (NKJV). This is another familiar scripture that we often quote. Yet, do we apply its instructions? Paul tells us to not be conformed to this world, or to not conform our lives or our mindsets in the fashion of the world. In society, just about anything goes. If it feels good, then do it. The world encourages any and everything, aside from holiness.

In consequence, Paul instructs us to be transformed, or changed, by renewing our mind. What does it mean to renew our minds and how do we do it? When we receive salvation, we have a change of heart and mind (deep beliefs). Our human nature desires to continue in the ways of sin; but we must retrain ourselves to desire the things of God.

The Christian walk is not a sprint, but it is a lifelong marathon. We must spend time in prayer and devotion each day to ensure that our spirit man remains dominant over our fleshly nature.

Mind renewal is essential to overriding distractions and developing in Kingdom principles. Think of renewing the mind as charging a cell phone. Most of us use our cell phones every day, all throughout the day. What happens if we go to sleep at night without having charged it? The next day will likely be frustrating because we will not begin the day with a full charge. We may even have a dead battery before lunch! The information or insight that we need most will not be accessible because we failed to charge.

The concept is the same with renewing our minds in the Spirit. We must be intentional to plug into our power source (the Word of God and the Holy Spirit) daily so that we may hear the voice of God clearly and walk in His ways. Failure to renew (recharge) our minds can cause us to focus on the wrong things, such as past failures, our enemies, unfortunate circumstances, or even a desperate cry for companionship instead of who God is, what He is able to do, and what we should be doing to advance the Kingdom.

We can also find ourselves embracing things and people that are not God-sent, even when we have the best of intentions. If you need motivation, then maintain at least one accountability partner that will help to steer you back to true north when you are going astray and will insist that you "stay focused and look forward."

Training Day 6

Faith It 'til You Make It

Most people that I have encountered in my daily life have had some exposure to the Gospel of Christ, whether they choose to believe the message or not. When having a conversation with a person about whether he or she is a Christian, most of the time the response is, "Yes." Furthermore, many church goers or believers affirm that they believe that Christ died, was buried, and rose again for the forgiveness of sins. However, the dilemma is that this is where most believers stop believing.

Faith is an essential component in the life of any believer and especially in the life of singles. Our God is wonderful and cares about each area of our lives, yes, even the desires for companionship. We must never limit Him or assume that He does not want us to be happy. Our faith must be developed in such a way that we are firm in every area of our lives, just as we are confident that we have received salvation. The Greek word for confession is homologéō, which means, in part, an emphatic declaration of truth.[16] Accordingly, our job is simply to say what God has said in His Word and apply it to each situation.

So then, faith comes from hearing the message, and
the message comes through preaching Christ.
Romans 10:17, GNB

I am so thankful that my parents and my pastors have taken the time to teach me how to apply the Word of faith to my daily life. The application of Romans 10:17 is very personal. This goes beyond merely attending church or listening to a sermon on a podcast, but it requires us to DO something, much like the man at the pool of Bethesda.

Do you desire to be made well? If so, then take up your bed and walk. Taking up your bed and walking in a spiritual sense indicates that you are no longer accepting the condition that your life is in, but that you are now determined to see change. You have received the Good News spoken to you, and you are putting that belief into action. You will not tolerate emotional turmoil and instability. Because you have changed your posture to that of a winner, you will not operate from a victim mentality. Additionally, you will dismiss the lies that you have nothing to offer or that no one desires you. At this very moment, you can make a choice.

So, how do you take up your bed and walk? By activating your faith. YOUR faith. Your faith will come alive when you hear your own voice speak the promises of God. We can go through our entire lives hearing the pastor say that God will provide for us, but until we make it our personal agenda to access faith, which is the currency of heaven, we will never be in position to receive the promises of God. Speaking God's Word must become second nature, like driving a car or brushing our teeth. Our lives must be hidden in Him and entrenched in faith.

But without faith, it is impossible to [walk with God
and] please Him, for whoever comes [near] to God must
[necessarily] believe that God exists, and that He rewards
those who [earnestly and diligently] seek Him.
Hebrews 11:6, AMP

Plainly put, we cannot please God if we do not have faith. The first step is to believe that God is real. The second step is to believe that He rewards those who seek His face. You can seek the Lord in prayer, meditation upon His Word, fasting, and in worship. During this quality time with Him, you will learn to hear His voice and you will grow to know His heart.

Faith is Kingdom Currency

Those who know me or even those who know of me are aware that I grew up in the church. For as long as I can recall, I heard the scripture quoted: "Now, faith is the substance of things hoped for, the evidence of things not seen" (Hebrews 11:1, NKJV). But what does this verse really mean when you are struggling to believe that God will grant your heart's desires and provide for you? What does this verse mean when you may be questioning whether God cares if you are truly happy in life? How is this scripture applicable when there is more month left at the end of your money? To bring it even closer to home, what does this passage mean when you have lost the love of your life, or when a relationship has been ripped apart and you feel the effects of it?

Most of us hear about faith but have yet to learn how to access and use it. As stated, faith is Kingdom currency, just like each country has its currency that is established by its government. The United States has the Dollar. Europe uses the Euro. Latin America uses the Peso, and so forth and so on.

> **Your faith will come alive when you hear your own voice speak the promises of God.**

In order to receive an exchange for goods or services sought, one must tender his currency. Not only must he tender currency, but he must tender the right currency in a particular country. If you ever go to a major city or overseas on a vacation, you will notice that there will be establishments labeled, "currency exchange," so that you are able to exchange your U.S. Dollars or whatever you have, for the currency of that country. This enables you to access goods and services.

Consider this example: I ordered some items online and a receipt was emailed with confirmation that the product would ship within three days. The moment I tendered my currency, was the moment I received what was rightfully mine. I was just waiting on its arrival. The receipt that I received in my email was proof that I had released my currency to access what I had requested. It was the "evidence" of what I hoped to receive.

The moment you release your faith is the moment at which you become the recipient of what you have petitioned God. Your personal belief is your confirmation email, or the "evidence" of what you have hoped for. All that is next is the manifestation; nevertheless, we cannot become discouraged between the releasing of faith and the manifestation. This is where we must endure and exercise faith and patience. The key to faith and patience is maintaining an attitude of thanksgiving and worship.

In one of my singles' Bible study sessions, I asked each student to write down her prayer requests. Once the requests were written, I provided each with an individual receipt that stated: "Request Granted." If you need a friendly reminder that God has answered your prayer, then make yourself a receipt as a reminder that your faith is working!

Faith and Patience Work Together

In the Old Testament, Daniel prayed for an answer from God. Twenty-one days later, he received the answer for which he prayed. The angel informed Daniel that his prayer was heard the moment he prayed, but that the princes of Persia (territorial demons) blocked the angel. Once Michael the archangel showed up on the scene, the angel was able to deliver Daniel's prayer request to him.[17] Sometimes as we exercise our faith, we may experience opposing forces. In spite of this, we must remember that God is all powerful and that we will always prevail.

When we pray, we must believe that we have received. Then we "wait" on the manifestation of the promise. What should we do while we wait? In addition to thanksgiving and worship, we should find ourselves serving. Another form of waiting is "serving." Who wouldn't want an opportunity to wait on royalty? People who serve in a royal palace count it an honor just to be in the presence of royalty. They receive the benefits of the royal ones just by being in their presence.

We should be found serving the King as we anticipate the fulfillment of His promises. Not only to get something, but because of our adoration towards Him. In the Book of Ezra, the children of Solomon's servants, who had lived with Solomon's family, esteemed it a great honor that they had been servants to so great a prince.[18] Likewise, we should be honored to serve and wait on our King!

In the Kingdom of God, each person has been given a measure of faith that we can freely use. Remember: when we go to God in prayer, we must believe that He exists, and that He is a rewarder of those that diligently seek Him. Next, we must believe that we have received what we ask the moment that we pray. I have found that most Christians assume that we have faith until we are caught in a holding pattern. Think of a holding pattern when a plane is attempting to land on the runway. If the runway is not clear, the plane must continue circling in the air until permitted to land.

Sometimes, it can feel like our lives are in holding patterns of waiting on the fulfillment of promises. We can feel as though we are spinning our wheels at full speed, but that we are getting nowhere. That is why faith and patience are complementary and must be exercised together. One without the other would bring strain. Faith without patience will wear down and diminish over time, causing us to lose confidence in God and His Word. Without patience, doubt begins to creep in. Once we give in to doubt, we are in danger of missing the promises.

> But let him ask in faith, with no doubting, for he who doubts
> is like a wave of the sea driven and tossed by the wind. For let
> not that man suppose that he will receive anything from the
> Lord; he is a double-minded man, unstable in all his ways.
> **James 1:6–8, NKJV**

When patience accompanies our faith, it takes us to a place of rest. We can rest on God's Word because we know that it shall not fail. "God is not a man that He should lie, nor a son of man, that He should repent. Has He said, and will not He do? Or has He spoken, and will He not make it good?" (Numbers 23:19, NKJV). The Word of God assures us that our Father is true to His Word and that He will do whatever He said He will do. When we develop a heightened sensitivity to the reality that God is true to His Word, then we will be more inclined to walk in our true identity as an heir of God.

I found that the more that my faith increased, I wanted to really live the life that God has made available for me to live, even down to doing a better job at keeping my own word. Perhaps we struggle with believing that God will keep His Word because we seldom keep ours!

> **Most of us hear about faith but have yet to learn how to access and use it.**

Now on the other hand, patience without faith can lead to passivity. There are some believers that are extremely passive in life and live by the "Que Sera Sera" principle ("whatever will be will be"). Patience is a virtue, but without the activation of faith, one would just be waiting on something that may or may not come into fruition.

Faith is Seed Sown

Faith is also our bag of seed. If you have a bit of a green thumb, you will recognize that sometimes the grass just won't grow and it needs some assistance so that it can grow to be thick, green and beautiful. To accomplish that, some may plant grass seed.

There are different types of grass seed that will accommodate a planter's desired outcome. If you live in a warm climate and want golf course type grass, you would plant the Bermuda grass seed to get that desired outcome. In the alternative, if you live in a cooler climate, you may consider using Fine Fescue grass seed because it tolerates shade well but does not tolerate heat very well.[19] The principle is the same in the Kingdom of God.

Along with your patience, you must activate your faith by fertilizing your field to reach the desired outcome. We fertilize our surroundings by what we say. What have you been saying? Have you been speaking negatively over your life, your circumstances, your relationships, or your future? Have you been saying things like, "I will never forgive that person," or "There aren't any good men/women around here," "I'll never meet anyone worth having," "Marriage is overrated," and "Nothing ever goes right for me"? If so, I implore you to repent this very moment and to negate every negative word spoken.

Believe it or not, you have been fertilizing your field, even if it is with the wrong type of seed. That is why it is essential that you study God's Word to discover what He says about you, your happiness, your desires, and your future so that you can repeat what He has said about you. Life and death are in the power of the tongue.

Not only is it necessary to properly plant the appropriate grass seed, it is also vital to ensure that the soil in your field is adequately prepared to receive the seed. Any rocks or debris that may be in the soil will prevent the grass seed from settling into the ground, causing the grass seed to blow or wash away. That is why we discussed on the previous training days that it is necessary to forgive those that have wronged us, forgive ourselves, and to even forgive God for what we believe are let-downs.

Our faith is ineffective if our hearts are not pure and free to love. Remember that faith works through love and they go hand in hand. God's love for us drives us to love Him in return and to trust Him more.

We then take on His character and extend that love to others. This is a winning combination to faith activation!

Once you have prepared your soil and properly spread the seed across the field, you must continue to water your field. This ensures that the grass roots grow down deep into the soil, rendering the desired result of healthy, full green grass. This process may not always yield the desired results as quickly as you prefer, but you must keep watering the seed. One lawn care company's slogan grabbed my attention because it stated: "With preparation, the right quality seeds, well-prepared soil, and a little patience, you can start a new lawn yourself."

> **Have you been speaking negatively over your life, your circumstances, your relationships, or your future?**

In the Kingdom of God, we prepare our hearts to receive when we keep our hearts pure and we then fertilize our field when we speak the promises of God. We must then water those seeds of faith with praise and thanksgiving. The more we praise God and thank Him in advance for what we have requested, the stronger our faith and expectancy will be. Praise is vital to the life of our seed so that the words of faith that we have spoken in our lives will be deeply rooted in the land on which we tread. Our praise is also the lifeline to our ability to exercise patience while waiting on the manifestation of the expected end.

Just as the planter cannot grow weary in well doing as he waters the seed in his field, we must continue to exercise faith and patience along with praise as we wait for the manifested promises of God. "And let us not grow weary while doing good, for in due season we shall reap if we do not lose heart" (Galatians 6:9, NKJV).

Isn't it reassuring to know that because of Christ, we have access to all the things of God? Jesus teaches about having faith quite a bit during his time of ministry. I venture to say that it is because He told us that the just shall live by faith; therefore, we would need constant reminders of how to access and apply His principles.

When we grasp the importance of faith and get it into our spirits, we will be elevated above circumstances that have caused us pain and disappointment. We will begin to realize that even though we may have been let down or have experienced some unfavorable events, God and His love outweigh what we have gone through. The following scriptures are a few of my go-to passages for a faith booster. These passages should ignite the flame of faith in your heart.

> Now to Him who is able to do exceedingly abundantly
> above all that we ask or think, according to the power
> that works in us, to Him be glory in the church by Christ
> Jesus to all generations, forever and ever. Amen.
> **Ephesians 3:20, NKJV**

> The Lord will perfect that which concerns me;
> Your mercy, O Lord, endures forever.
> **Psalm 138:8a–b, NKJV**

Most assuredly, I say to you, he who believes in Me, the works
that I do he will do also; and greater works than these he
will do, because I go to My Father. And whatever you ask
in My name, that I will do, that the Father may be glorified
in the Son. If you ask anything in My name, I will do it.
John 14:12–14, NKJV

And Abraham believed the Lord, and the Lord
counted him as righteous because of his faith.
Genesis 15:6, NLT

Be on your guard; stand firm in the faith; be
courageous; be strong. Do everything in love.
I Corinthians 16:13–14, NIV

ROUND 3

You're doing great! You'll be looking and feeling just like a champ in no time!

Sink Yourself and Find Fulfillment

The next steps on the road to bringing our lives into alignment with God is to discover and begin walking in purpose. Galatians 6:4 states, "Make a careful exploration of who you are and the work that you have been given and sink yourself into that" (MSG). To explore indicates to go into unfamiliar territory to discover something or to gain information or knowledge.

Have you discovered what you're here for? Each of us has been placed here for a reason that will bring Glory to our Father. As mentioned early on, we are God's masterpieces, according to Ephesians 2:10. Everyone will not stand in the pulpit or on a platform, but we all have specific assignments that only we can do.

It is so refreshing to know that God is concerned about me fulfilling my purpose and that He will provide the tools, know-how, knowledge, and grace to get it all done. We all have certain qualities about us that give us a leg up in various areas in which we are assigned. Even though we may have deficiencies in our human nature, the Spirit of God within us always makes up for the lack thereof.

If we could do everything in our own strength, we would not need

God's power. Check out what He did in the Old Testament. In Exodus, God wanted a tabernacle built under Moses's leadership. So, God hand-picked some men to do the job just as He wanted it done.

> The Lord spoke to Moses, saying: See, I have called by name Bezalel
> the son of Uri,…And I have filled him with the Spirit of God, in
> wisdom, in understanding, in knowledge, and in all manner of
> workmanship, to design artistic works, to work in gold, in silver, in
> bronze, in cutting jewels for setting, in carving wood, and to work
> in all manner of workmanship. And I, indeed, I, have appointed
> with him Aholiab …and I have put wisdom in the hearts of all the
> gifted artisans, that they may make all that I have commanded you.
> **Exodus 31:1–6, NKJV**

Isn't it amazingly reassuring to know that God will equip us to do what He has called us to do? Your confidence should have just risen by about 10 notches since you know that the Lord will give you the tools necessary to carry out His will. We all have moments in which we may feel inadequate, but in those moments of weakness is when He is made strong within us.

If you have not asked the Lord to show you your purpose, I challenge you to do so now. You may be working on a job that is not fulfilling to you. Is that where God wants you to be? Do you have a burning desire deep within to acquire another degree or to go obtain a certification? If so, God is letting you know that what you sense deep inside has to do with your purpose.

My pastors would often ask our congregation, "What are you willing to do without receiving any compensation for doing it?" Whatever the answer is, that is your passion. Whatever burning desires you have within your heart to do for God will lead you to your purpose.

There are people in the world that need what you have. You are equipped with special gifts that provide the solutions to unanswered problems. Never believe the lie that your life is insignificant and do not compare yourself to others. Your responsibility is to be the best version of yourself that you can possibly be. The trauma that you

> **We all have moments in which we may feel inadequate, but in those moments of weakness is when He is made strong within us.**

have experienced can be a ploy of the enemy to stop what God wants to accomplish in your life. That is why it is a must that you do not get stuck in a moment, but that you reach toward destiny.

> *Yet, what we suffer now is nothing compared to the glory he*
> *will reveal to us later. For all creation is waiting eagerly for that*
> *future day when God will reveal who his children really are.*
> **Romans 8:18–19, NLT**

All of creation is waiting for the manifestation of the sons of God. The world needs what you have, and someone's future is tied to your willingness to be the person that you were put on earth to be. What will you do about it?

My Path to Destiny

In 2014, I launched my outreach ministry, Passion For Purpose. Initially, I was doubtful about the name because to me, it did not flow. Conversely,

God let me know that it was not about popularity or sounding catchy, but that the sole point of the ministry is to encourage men and women to discover and fulfill their purpose.

After I launched the ministry, there were periods in which it lay dormant because of the events that I was experiencing. Every now and then, I would hear the word "passion" or even the word "purpose" and it would make me cringe because I knew that I had placed my God-given baby on the shelf. I was attempting to tune it out, but I did not have peace.

Once I decided to realign my focus and step back into obedience, I began to experience the peace of God as never before. This does not mean that everything was peaches and cream, but God had given me a resolve that He would take care of me through every challenge as I pursue His will. When we tap into our passions that lead to our purpose, we will be on target to receive the manifested blessings of God. Our purpose and our desire to please the Father should steer our lives and daily decisions, emotional trauma should not.

If you are still uncertain about what your gifts, talents, passions and purpose is, then I suggest that you get involved with a community organization or a local church so that you can serve others with accountability. You may also consider taking the Myers-Briggs Type Indicator test that breaks down personalities and provides insight on which career choices are best suited for certain personality types. You can learn more about personality types and how they affect our life choices in "People Patterns" by Dr. Steven Montgomery, in which he examines how personalities are connected to career paths, mate selection, and raising children.[20] It is also beneficial to take a spiritual gifts assessment to determine what your spiritual gifts may be or in what areas you may be best suited.

The personality assessment will provide excellent insight so that we understand ourselves and others better; then again, we cannot limit our purpose and call to our personality traits. God may place us in an area of ministry that takes us totally out of our comfort zone.

If your local church does not have these materials, then check at a local library or online for these self-assessment tools. In addition to utilizing those tools, you must earnestly pray and ask God to reveal your purpose to you. If you are willing to listen, He will speak. Partnering with a mentor who is walking in a similar calling is extremely vital so that you can learn. Being passionate about your gifts and callings is wonderful, until you execute in ignorance. You want to ensure that you are going about things according to God's instructions and not your own ideology.

It is OK if you are not sure what your purpose is right now. On the contrary, you should never sit idly by because there is much to be done. While you serve, you will discover your talents, gifts, and your calling and you will develop a heart of compassion. This is the means by which you will experience peace within.

Fulfillment, in its truest form, is realized when you are operating in your purpose. A God-given companion is wonderful; yet, God will still hold us accountable for fulfilling our destiny whether we have a companion or not. The Scripture tells us that upon marriage, the two shall become one. In view of

> **A God-given companion is wonderful; yet, God will still hold us accountable for fulfilling our destiny whether we have a companion or not.**

that, it is imperative to have a likeminded companion that will accommodate our purpose.

A challenging feat is to have selected a spouse based on a temporary feeling and then later discover your purpose. I have seen some marriages experience conflict because one begins to discover who he or she is truly meant to be, and the other person does not agree nor understand. This is not in every case, but it is wise to spare ourselves the friction and conflict by walking in purpose during the single season so that we can cross paths with a mate who will complement and not hinder us while on the road to destiny.

God is a multifaceted and brilliant God. He may want you to own your own business, run for public office, be a physician or a pastor. Whatever the path is that you are called to, do what it takes to prepare. Invest in yourself and your future.

Some of my friends have jokingly called me weird and I was on the verge of believing them. As a child, I knew that I wanted to be an attorney, even though I had never met an attorney and had never sat in a courtroom. The closest I had gotten was watching everyone's favorite television mom, Claire Huxtable on "The Cosby Show." I believe that God allowed those seeds to be planted. Not only that, but as I grew up, the seeds of business and leadership were planted.

I am grateful and honored that God saw fit to equip me with so many gifts and talents. Throughout high school, the Lord blessed me to maintain over a 4.1 grade point average and to graduate with high honors. I then attended college on a full scholarship and held various leadership roles in my sorority, Alpha Kappa Alpha, and in the College of Business. I traveled across the country to represent my college in business development competitions. After college, I attended law school and was once again favored with leadership responsibilities. Many of these opportunities were thrust upon me because of the favor that rested on my life.

After my law school matriculation, a door was opened for me to relocate to Chicago, Illinois, in 2007. Because of the economic downturn, the career opportunities that I thought would be there were cut short. Nonetheless, God opened doors for me to gain favor with attorneys and prominent people in the city.

One of my acquired mentors, Attorney Lester Barclay, was extremely instrumental. I had the occasion to meet politicians, T.V. personalities, and represented high profile clients (whose names will remain undisclosed). Although my time in Chicago was short lived because of a failing economy, I am thankful for the experience in that I developed tenacity, independence, and character.

A couple of years went by and I returned to Arkansas. I was a bit discouraged because I dreaded starting over in my career. Nonetheless, I attained my Arkansas law license and began practicing again after a brief stint of teaching at a local community college. The Lord showed Himself faithful once again by opening doors and placing favorable opportunities in my lap.

A few years later in 2014, I was selected as the Chair of the Young Lawyers' Section of the Arkansas Bar Association. This meant that I would lead all lawyers under the age of 36 in the State of Arkansas and would

> **I was still pursuing the purpose that God gave me.**

be responsible for planning meetings, overseeing a budget, and helping to implement legislation. It would also mean that once again, I would be traveling across the country to represent Arkansas on a national level within the American Bar Association. Who would have thought that a young girl from El Dorado, Arkansas, would be in a position to reserve a skybox suite at a professional baseball game for her peers and colleagues?

I realize that God handpicked me for this journey. While my friends were getting married and having children, I was still pursuing the purpose that God gave me. The same is true today. While I desire to experience the joys of marriage and children, I can still experience fulfillment until the season for marriage and children comes.

My career path has been everything but easy and straight. I have had many lonely nights, busy days, and days in which I wanted to be invisible. However, I recognized that the tests and trials only made me stronger. We must expect obstacles while on the road to destiny. Tribulation does not equate to the absence of favor. Many times, it is an indication that you are headed in the right direction.

I take no credit for the favor of God on my life, yet I also make no apologies for it. When you tap into your divine purpose, the doors of favor will fling open and nothing will be able to stop the move of God. Since that time, I have continued to practice law in Arkansas and have worked alongside various politicians and public servants to discover how best to increase economic surplus and enhance the quality of life in various communities.

I have had occasions to run for public office and have had high profile politicians to personally meet with me and ask that I do so. But the Lord instructed me to wait. I also sought wise counsel from my pastors and the Lord confirmed through them that I should wait.

I will remain sensitive to His voice so that when the time comes, I will be ready to execute. I have several goals and visions that I am continuing to work toward. It is important to move in the right season. Having a baby prematurely may be detrimental to the baby because his organs are not fully developed to handle the elements of the environment. Likewise, delaying delivery can cause complications because the mother's body is seeking to eject a foreign object that is fully developed but unwilling to be released.

I am continuing to invest in myself and plan for the future. When I depart this life, I want to have touched every person and impacted each community that God instructed me to. What are you doing to serve humanity?

I am also grateful that my parents were alert and aware to ensure that my gifts were cultivated and not stifled. While they encouraged us to excel in school, they admonished us to serve the Lord. They bought various instruments for my brothers and me and encouraged us to sing and play music. As we got older, we were all musically inclined and supplied the singing and music for my father's church. My parents had a heart for ministry and deposited the same seeds within us.

These seeds that my parents planted brought forth a harvest rather quickly. I preached my first official sermon at the age of 19 and began facilitating revivals shortly thereafter. God had a magnificent call on my life, but my parents were responsible for planting the right seeds during my childhood. If you have children, make it a point to notice what their gifts and talents are. Allow the Lord to speak to your heart so that you can steer them toward Kingdom purpose at an early age.

Human Needs Analysis

When we finally tap into our purpose, we will experience a supernatural satisfaction. Are you familiar with Abraham Maslow? He was a psychologist that formulated the hierarchy of five categories of human needs. He diagramed these needs in the form of a pyramid. At the bottom of Maslow's original diagram, he included physiological needs, which would include food and clothing, then safety and security, love and social needs, esteem needs, and then self-actualization needs atop the pyramid. See the illustration.[21]

Maslow couples his work with that of Sigmund Freud, mentioned previously. According to Maslow, when one level of need is met, an individual progresses to the next higher level of need as a form of motivation.[22] So, for instance, if you feel that your love or social needs are met, you will advance internally to acquire esteem needs.

Maslow's theory is that we are motivated by needs and once certain needs are met, we are then motivated to pursue the next one in the hierarchy. Some scientists disagree with Maslow's theory because some people progress in different patterns. For example, one person may pursue esteem needs before pursuing safety and security, or he may pursue self-actualization needs while pursuing love (social needs). Both perspectives bring plausible arguments to the table. Nonetheless, the ultimate consensus is that we are all wired with similar needs.

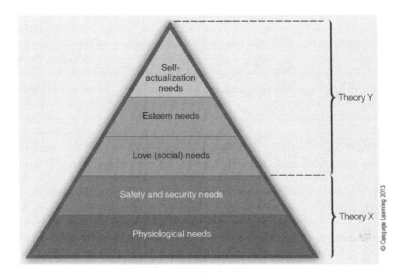

While we are all wired with similar needs, it must be noted that in the Kingdom of God, we do not live our lives in a needs-driven fashion. The purpose of this illustration is to show the nature of the basic needs of man and how Maslow identified self-actualization as the utmost need for mankind. As Kingdom citizens, we live by faith. Because we live by faith, we do not have to allow ourselves to be consumed with seeking out the fulfillment of every little need. All we have to do is ask and receive.

> And my God will supply all your needs according
> to His riches in glory in Christ Jesus.
> **Philippians 4:19, NASB**

Notice that atop of Maslow's original pyramid are self-actualization needs, which focus on achieving one's maximum potential.[23] Many times, we are guilty of attempting to substitute the fulfillment of certain needs. We may attempt to fulfill the self-actualization needs with the love/social resources. While I do not agree with all of Maslow's views, I would venture to say that he was not too far off the grid when he placed self-actualization atop the original pyramid. (He changed it slightly just before he died to add ethics to the top.)

God created us with an innate desire to pursue our purpose in the earth and to bring Glory to Him. Only the Lord can satisfy the fulfillment of certain needs. That is why so many individuals are left desiring more even after acquiring material things and companionship. We are made in His image and likeness. Thus, our spirit longs to rise within us, to achieve, to accomplish, and to create good things, realizing our maximum potential. We were created to have dominion in the earth. When God created the heavens and earth, He gave Himself the credit and recognized that it was "good."

For in him all things were created: things in heaven and on earth, visible and invisible, whether thrones or powers or rulers or authorities; all things have been created through him and for him.
Colossians 1:16, NIV

Remember what God told Adam while he was in the Garden? He was to have dominion on the earth and to rule. After Adam sinned and fell from Grace, Jesus came to restore us back to our rightful place so that we can now have dominion and rule on the earth. We were made to reign and rule. This is our true identity and fulfillment will not be maximized until we discover and walk in who God created us to be. Recall what we discussed earlier about how all of creation is waiting on the manifestation of the Children of God.

Yet, what we suffer now is nothing compared to the glory he
will reveal to us later. For all creation is waiting eagerly for that
future day when God will reveal who his children really are.
Romans 8:18–19, NLT

In other words, it is time for all of us to be who God created us to be and to do what He created us to do. I am qualified to write these things concerning singleness because I am walking out the process just as you are. By sinking myself into purpose, I know that for the God-sent mate to find me, He will have sunk himself into his purpose, too. Until that time, I am enjoying a fulfilled life. Challenges and obstacles still come in my life now, but I am confident that God has already provided the victory. It is my duty to look for the footprints that He has laid out before me and to walk toward destiny.

Because I am experiencing genuine fulfillment during my single season, when the season for marriage comes, I will not place upon my mate an unfair expectation to fill certain voids. Even if you are at a place in life in which you have decided to remain single, you must still make certain that an undue burden to fill certain voids is not unfairly placed upon family and friends. There is a place in all our hearts that only God can fill. When we pursue His purpose for our lives wholeheartedly, He will not leave us empty, but we will experience the love, peace, happiness and fulfillment that only God our Father can give.

May the God of hope fill you with all joy and peace
as you trust in Him, so that you may overflow
with hope by the power of the Holy Spirit.
Romans. 15:13, NIV

Training Day 8

Maintain Joy and Create Happiness

It is a wonderful feeling to know that I am walking in my true calling and am doing what God has commanded of me. Once you sink yourself into your purpose, genuine fulfillment will follow. While we as singles desire a meaningful relationship, there is a particular fulfillment that comes from operating in purpose that a relationship cannot yield.

Of course, there are challenges and brief moments of loneliness; but, because we are operating in our assignment, we will not be overtaken in loneliness or despair. Every day will not be perfect and there will be trials and conflicts. Oftentimes, challenges arise merely because you are making an impact for the Kingdom of God. Nonetheless, this genuine and supernatural fulfillment makes joy, happiness, and contentment come more naturally. God provides the joy through His Word, His promises, and through our relationship with Him and He has given us the tools to create our own worlds of happiness.

You will show me the path of life; in Your presence is fullness of joy, at your right hand there are pleasures forevermore.
Psalm 16:11, AMPC

If you are born again, then the source of your joy comes from the Holy Spirit. Joy is gladness of heart, while happiness is a mental state of being. There are tons of happy people in the world, but that does not mean that they have Christ. Unholy things can make a person happy. In contrast, for the believer, not only do we have access to happiness, but we also have access to the fruits of the Spirit, which include joy. If one has accepted Christ, joy should be a part of his new nature, just as love and peace should be.

The Joy of the Lord

There are several instances of joy in Scripture, accompanied by rejoicing in the Lord's goodness. Pleasures in life should bring us joy, such as healthy relationships, marriages, childbirths and graduations. These are often identified as joyous occasions, and rightfully so. In addition to those momentous moments, we should always look to God to be the ultimate source of our joy.

Consider again Psalm 16, in which David expressed his confidence in Almighty God. He understood that the full extent of the gladness of his heart was connected to God's presence. Notice that despite all of David's challenges throughout Scripture, he maintained the heart of worship toward God. The key to maintaining our joy in the season of singleness is to perfect our life of worship. When we worship something, it means that we are giving the object of such worship due reverence and adoration by kneeling before it and paying homage.[24] What is it that you adore? A cute baby in the grocery store? Your significant other? Your car? Whatever it is that you adore on earth, you should adore the Lord 100 times more. Consider what Jesus told the woman that was caught in adultery:

But an hour is coming, and is now here, when the true worshipers
will worship the Father in spirit and truth. God is spirit, and
those who worship Him must worship in spirit and truth.
John 4:23–24, HCSB [25]

Jesus was letting the woman know that God is a Spirit and that true worshipers must worship Him in Spirit, regardless of location. The Samaritan woman had knowledge that her forefathers worshiped on Mount Gerizim, the place where Jesus met her, and that the Jews worshiped in Jerusalem. [26] Conversely, the true worshiper would not limit his worship to a location but would carry the spirit of worship in all places and at all times. Hence, the key to maintaining joy in a world of chaos and turmoil is to be a consistent and authentic worshiper.

The means by which we can discover the awesome facets of our God is to spend quality time with Him and to meditate upon His Word. It would be quite difficult to come to truly adore someone with whom you rarely spend time. Additionally, quality time with God allows us to experience His power and His amazing Grace, making it extremely easy to fall in love with who He is.

I'm sure that you have been in love. It is as if there is a glow that springs forth from within that even strangers may notice. "You sure are glowing!" I've heard that statement before. That glow also comes about when we have tapped into the supernatural joy of the Lord. It does not mean that you have become "churchy" or "really religious," as some would assume. It means that you have finally connected with the source of true and everlasting joy that the world cannot give or take away.

Remember that God is love. So, imagine experiencing love in its most perfect form. The love of God is perfect; therefore, we are bound to experience the fullness of joy in the presence of God, of which David spoke. In addition, consider the words of Apostle Paul:

> May you, having been [deeply] rooted and [securely] grounded in love, be fully capable of comprehending with all the saints (God's people) the width and length and height and depth of His love [fully experiencing that amazing, endless love]; and [that you may come] to know [practically, through personal experience] the love of Christ which far surpasses [mere] knowledge [without experience], that you may be filled up [throughout your being] to all the fullness of God [so that you may have the richest experience of God's presence in your lives, completely filled and flooded with God Himself].
> **Ephesians 3:17b–19, AMP**

Paul was letting the church at Ephesus know that God's love for us is endless and His love surpasses all knowledge and wisdom. The love of God extends as far back as we can fathom (and beyond), and as far in the future as we can imagine (and beyond). God's gift in the form of His son Jesus was an expression of His love for us and He wants us to experience that perfect love for ourselves. By experiencing this perfect love, we also have access to the presence of God that dwells within us. If we are filled and flooded with God Himself, it would be impossible not to live a life of overwhelming fulfillment, joy, and peace!

Practice Being Happy

Once we begin to truly understand who God is and accept His love for us, we should find ourselves engaging in a lifestyle of worship and adoration. This mode of worship will invite His presence into our lives, our homes, and each circumstance, and will create an atmosphere conducive for miracles, signs, and wonders. Furthermore, we will experience the fullness of joy that cannot be erased based upon outside circumstances. This joy will come from within and allow us to create an atmosphere of happiness.

In one of my singles' Bible study sessions, I asked the students if they believed that God wants them to be happy. Some of them said yes, while others hesitated. Well, the truth of the matter is that God wants you to be happy! Happiness is a state of being or a mindset that we can

> **If one has accepted Christ, joy should be a part of his new nature, just as love and peace should be.**

choose to have in each stage of our lives. We can maintain this state of being happy throughout our life's processes, whether circumstances are favorable or not.

We must be careful not to predicate happiness upon reaching a certain place or acquiring certain things. How many times have you made similar statements to what I've made? "I will be happy when …," "I would be happy if …" Well, believe it or not, you can think yourself into happiness. It is all about perspective.

One time I was in a therapy session and my therapist (who was also a Christian) told me to look at each situation by utilizing the "beach ball approach." This approach means that when faced with an obstacle, that one must have the ability to look at the situation from a different perspective. Picture a beach ball. If two people are standing on opposite sides of the ball, one person may see the colors blue, purple and red, while the person on the other side may see the colors orange, yellow, and green. Neither of them is lying about what color the ball is; it's just that their perspectives are different.

Consequently, it may be true that your working environment is a hostile one, or that you are not paid your worth. It may also be true that your life has been subpar in the relationship department; still, take the time to consider the positives that spring forth out of these unfavorable circumstances because things could always be worse. These types of unfavorable situations present perfect opportunities for God to show Himself strong on behalf of those that love Him.

Let's take another look at Apostle Paul, for instance. In the Book of Acts, he had been taken into custody and the Jews had a very strong desire to kill him because he had questioned their laws. Paul's accusers sought to charge him for agitating the Jews and attempted to present evidence to the governor. Paul continued preaching the Gospel and told the Jews that even though Jesus had been crucified, that He was now alive. He was held in prison unjustly for about two years because there was insufficient evidence that warranted putting him to death.

> By experiencing this perfect love, we also have access to the presence of God that dwells within us.

In Chapter 26, Paul was standing before King Agrippa and was permitted to speak on his own behalf. Although Paul was bound in chains and was standing before someone who had the authority to place him on death row, he answered in the following manner:

"I think myself happy, King Agrippa, because today I shall
answer for myself before you concerning all the things of which
I am accused by the Jews, especially because you are expert in
all customs and questions which have to do with the Jews ..."
Acts 26:2–3, NKJV

Paul's response begs the question: Why would he be happy or consider himself fortunate in such an ugly scene? He had been in prison, he was wrongfully accused, and there were people that wanted him dead. Paul could have easily "thought" himself into suicide, depression and anxiety. Instead, he was happy because of what he knew. He knew that although his circumstances were dreadful, that God was with him and was orchestrating favor.

Notice that Paul did not wait until he was released from prison to think himself into happiness. He did so while bound in chains. Paul was becoming famous as the witness of Jesus to those in authority. People had heard about him all throughout Judea, Samaria, Syria and other countries, and so the king was curious to hear what he would say.[27]

When we are settled into our rightful places, there is a level of peace that our minds reach, and that place is beyond mediocrity. We will often discover that the things or people that we thought we needed in order to be happy are not as important or significant as we once thought. The steps that we have previously covered are vital in reaching this point at which you are able to create your own happy place. What does happiness look like to you while living single? Whatever environment you deem to be a happy and peaceful one, you have the power to create it, even in the face of adversity. It does not have to be anything overly complicated.

I found my happy place in writing this book and thinking about all the hearts that would be encouraged and the lowered heads that would be lifted. Other ways in which I create happiness is by doing things that I enjoy, such as going to a movie and enjoying a bucket of popcorn. I also pulled out my paint brushes and canvases and created some works of art. Listening to jazz music or something smooth while riding down the highway puts a smile on my face. In some of my past relationships, I pushed my own happiness to the side in order to accommodate someone else's. One should never stop being an individual and doing the wholesome things that bring peace in order to sustain a relationship.

Happiness could look totally different for you in this season than it does for me. However you see it in your heart, pursue it. Ask God to grant you wisdom in creating your own mindset of happiness that permeates and radiates to those around you. Find ways to be thankful each day, whether it is for the sunshine or for a great parking spot at work. It would be difficult to remain unhappy if you are maintaining a heart of thanksgiving.

> "Don't mourn or weep on such a day as this! For today is a sacred day before the Lord your God. Go and celebrate with a feast of rich foods and sweet drinks, and share gifts of food with people who have nothing prepared. This is a sacred day before our Lord. Don't be dejected and sad, for the joy of the Lord is your strength!"
> **Nehemiah 8:9b, 10, NLT**

When we understand that God's joy is what gives us strength from day to day, we will put less emphasis on people, places, and material things. A key component in defeating heartbreak and growing stronger each day is through living a lifestyle of praise and thanksgiving. This mindset elevates us above unfavorable circumstances and cantankerous people.

Protect Your Happy Place

One reason why it is vitally important for singles that have experienced heartbreak to overcome is because heartbroken people have the tendency to become bitter if forgiveness is not employed. Holding on to offenses creates a bigger mountain of unforgiveness in the heart, which is why we are instructed in Proverbs 4:23, "Above all else, guard your heart, for everything you do flows from it" (NIV). In other words, if you have an issue in your heart against someone, it is going to come out in some fashion.

If you harbor unforgiveness, it will be difficult to live in true happiness because oftentimes bitterness produces cynicism. A cynic is a fault-finding critic.[28] Have you ever heard someone make a sarcastic comment with a smile on his or her face? The comment is borderline offensive, but the person persists that it was all a joke. That is an example of a cynical person. They are pessimistic and many times, do not trust other people and refuse to see the good in situations. These individuals that eject venomous statements do not realize that they have become toxic and are polluting the environment around them.

True happiness cannot live in a cynical environment. That's why all residue of resentment must be released. It may not leave all at once, but as we receive God's Grace daily, we can forgive those that have caused us harm so that we do not become bitter and cynical.

In order to attract someone else that is walking in wholeness and emotional freedom, we must carry the spirit of joy and happiness. Remember that Christ has given us the oil of joy for sadness. It is up

> **If you harbor unforgiveness, it will be difficult to live in true happiness because oftentimes bitterness produces cynicism.**

to us to maintain what He has given. Our positive mindsets and outlooks on life should be infectious.

Sometimes, we may even draw people to us who are broken and are not yet on the road to wholeness. In those times, we should strive to inspire, but be careful to protect our environment of peace and happiness. We cannot always afford to be someone else's lifeline when we are striving for wholeness ourselves.

We must also be careful not to lose ourselves in pursuing relationships. Remember that any relationship that is sustained by your inability to be an individual or to maintain your own place of happiness is unhealthy. This is a perfect recipe for toxicity that may not be immediately apparent, but it would have the ability to fester over time. You will eventually tire of sacrificing your own happiness for the sake of someone else's if the demands are unreasonable. Unhappy people put strains on relationships, whether familial, platonic, or romantic in nature.

As you grow stronger every single day, learn to create your own happiness. Happiness that depends totally upon uncontrollable variables, such as other people, their presence, or material possessions is superficial. Why? Because when those people or things leave, so does the "happiness." These things should add to the happiness that you have already created. Let your happiness come from within. Be your own constant, resting in the consistency of the Father. He will be ever present.

Keep your lives free from the love of money and be content with what you have, because God has said, "Never will I leave you; never will I forsake you." So we say with confidence, "The Lord is my helper; I will not be afraid. What can mere mortals do to me?"
Hebrews 13:5–6, NIV

Imagine how beautiful it will be when your happiness collides with someone else's. That is a recipe for success with a high probability that the two will one day create a happy home. Other people and things should only add to our happiness, rather than be the sole source of it. Individuals that are operating in purpose will experience joy and are equipped with the tools to create happiness. Like Paul, you can maintain joy and think yourself happy!

ROUND 4

OK, now it's time to pull out all the stops.
Show me what you know!

Training Day 9

Next

I f you desire marriage as I do, then operating in purpose will bring us closer to destiny than you may realize. Even for those that do not desire marriage at this point in life, operating in purpose solidifies self-fulfillment and glorifies God in every way. While pursuing purpose, God begins to develop our character and we then increase in love and understanding. It is advantageous to fine tune our love-walk and compassion while in the single season so that it will not be a complete culture shock upon entering covenant. This is the best opportunity to be perfected in obedient grace, quickly hearing and following the Lord's instructions to us.

As we discussed on Training Day 8, the joy of the Lord is our strength. We are empowered when we are in the presence of God. When we live our lives in the presence of God and by walking in the Spirit, we will avoid the pitfalls of our fleshly nature. It is vital that we plow the field and do the groundwork in maturing in discernment and in reaching toward wholeness.

The next seasons of our lives will be more rewarding if we embark upon them in wholeness of mind, body, soul, and spirit. It is possible that you may encounter someone along the journey that piques your interest. By utilizing the training techniques contained within this book, as well as other strategies that may work for you, you will be more equipped to identify dysfunctional situations. At that point, it is up to you to employ sound judgement concerning where the relationship should lead.

You may be a healing agent for your soulmate (who is still struggling with past hurts). God may use you as an instrument to bring forth healing into someone else's life. That person may be your soulmate, but make sure the connection is of God. As a result of this training, you will be better equipped to use wisdom and gauge when the friendship should progress into a dating relationship or marriage to avoid pitfalls and unnecessary conflicts. It is not uncommon for people to be ready for a relationship in their heads, yet their hearts may still be damaged from past hurts.

Conquer the Desires for the Forbidden

Another extremely important step that we as singles should make in this season is to take this time to conquer the desires for the forbidden things. Some relationships fail because single people bring bad habits or strongholds into relationships and marriages, such as sexual perversion, selfishness, and dishonesty. Now is the time to master the fleshly desires and mature in discipline. Saying "I do" will not get rid of strongholds and bad habits no more than saying "Beetlejuice" will cause a guy in a black and white suit to appear in mid-air.

I urge you—don't allow yourself to become so comfortable and familiar with obscenities and vulgarity that you fail to guard your ear and eye gates. You must protect your environment so that it does not become contaminated. Have you ever gone to a store or to a restaurant where they played music? Sometimes, you may not be actively listening to what is playing, yet when you leave that location and arrive elsewhere, you find yourself singing the song that was playing, but you cannot recall where you heard it. The same can happen in other forms if we do not guard our minds and spirits from unwholesome things.

Recall that on Training Day 3, we covered some vital material that dealt with sexual sins. We discussed what Paul told the church at Corinth and Thessalonica, that we should run away from sexual immorality

We are empowered when we are in the presence of God.

because our bodies belong to Christ. That part is pretty cut and dried. However, what happens when we as singles are tempted to make adjustments in order to satisfy certain urges?

Many people, including members of the clergy, have made exceptions for pornography and masturbation. These are other areas that single believers should avoid. Some believe that these are safe mechanisms by which to satisfy sexual urges. Some may also suggest that since the Bible does not specifically say that pornography, foreplay and masturbation are wrong, that they are acceptable. But then again, consider the spirit and motivation behind the acts. If we cannot bring our bodies under subjection in the single season, then we may risk falling prey to outside temptation after entering a marriage covenant. Consider the following:

> You have heard the commandment that says, "You must not commit adultery." But I say, anyone who even looks at a woman with lust has already committed adultery with her in his heart.
> **Matthew 5:27–28, NLT**

*Do not let sin control the way you live; do not give in to sinful
desires. Do not let any part of your body become an instrument
of evil to serve sin. Instead, give yourselves completely to God,
for you were dead, but now you have new life. So use your whole
body as an instrument to do what is right for the glory of God.*
Romans 6:12–13, NLT

Once again, I have to refer to my guy, Apostle Paul. Take a look at
what he told the church at Corinth on another occasion:

*Some of you say, "We can do anything we want
to." But I tell you not everything is good for us. So
I refuse to let anything have power over me.*
I Corinthians 6:12, CEV

The key is discipline. Discipline is applicable across various sectors of life.
I remember when I played high school basketball. I hated off-season practice
because it was extremely hot, and we spent a lot of time running. We would
run through neighborhoods and up and down hilly streets. Of course, my
thoughts were, "I wish we could just go back to the gym so we can shoot and
play a scrimmage game." The coach knew that we would have plenty of time
to perfect our skills. In crunch time, skills would not be the issue. The issue
would be whether we would have the endurance, stamina, and mental fortitude to outhustle the other team. Skill would not matter if we did not have
the strength or conditioning to perform over a long period of time.

We had to accept that the off-season training was just as important
as the regular season games. Whatever we did or did not do during
training would show up during game time. By the same token, whatever

areas we do not master as singles will show up in the next season of marriage if it is to be desired.

Remember as we discussed during the Warm-Up on Training Day 1, that in order to be an effective boxer, boxers must undergo strenuous training that attacks individual areas of the body, while also promoting the technical skills of the sport. The same is true for Christian singles. Consider this time as "off-season" training.

It is beneficial that we learn to operate in obedience, self-control, and temperance in this single season. We must learn to be obedient to God's voice and steer clear of sexual sins and other forbidden things that our flesh may long for. It is imperative that we do this, so that when the season for marriage arrives, we will not be lured away by other temptations, but we will have conditioned ourselves to operate in discipline. Now is the time to strengthen the muscles of our Spirit so that we will not be lured away and enticed by our own lusts. Living by these principles will also help us to avoid some of the pitfalls that we may have previously gotten ourselves into that resulted from making fleshly decisions.

Some may believe that upon marriage, one would no longer be tempted sexually. Except, I believe that sometimes it is not the act of sex that tempts individuals, but it is the thrill and the secrecy that entices people to make poor choices. It has been in man's sinful nature to desire the things that are forbidden.

> **Now is the time to strengthen the muscles of our Spirit so that we will not be lured away and enticed by our own lusts.**

Consider what we discussed about Adam and Eve. They had the entire Garden at their disposal, except they were not to eat of the tree of the knowledge of good and evil. This is equivalent to individuals having a loving spouse at home, yet they are lured away and enticed by their own lusts. The serpent convinced Eve that God was not telling her the whole truth about the tree and that triggered her curiosity. The forbidden thing was the thing that they wanted.

> Now the serpent was more crafty than any of the wild animals
> the Lord God had made. He said to the woman, "Did God really
> say, 'You must not eat from any tree in the garden?'" The woman
> said to the serpent, "We may eat fruit from the trees in the
> garden, but God did say, 'You must not eat fruit from the tree
> that is in the middle of the garden, and you must not touch it, or
> you will die.'" "You will not certainly die," the serpent said to the
> woman. "For God knows that when you eat from it your eyes will
> be opened, and you will be like God, knowing good and evil."
> **Genesis 3:1–5, NIV**

Notice that the serpent questions Eve knowing that he is insinuating that God said that they couldn't eat from any tree in the garden. Then, Eve responds with improper information because God's instructions never indicated that they would die upon touching the tree, only upon eating from it. Satan has a way of luring us away by deception and then once we have cooperated, he leaves us standing there with our pants down. (Pun intended.) It is the sinful nature of man to go against the orders of God. Eve's conversation with the serpent led to compromising thoughts. Consequently, she believed the lie and made adjustments to

STRONGER EVERY SINGLE DAY

God's Word to accommodate her desire for the forbidden. Let's analyze further.

> So when the woman saw that the tree was good for food,
> that it was pleasant to the eyes, and a tree desirable to make
> one wise, she took of its fruit and ate. She gave also to her
> husband with her, and he ate. Then the eyes of both of them
> were opened, and they knew that they were naked; and they
> sewed fig leaves together and made themselves coverings.
> **Genesis 3:6–7, NKJV**

We should consider that the serpent's approach to Eve painted a picture of God that would suggest that he was strict and was impinging upon their freedom in the garden. This is an absurd notion because God had freely given Adam and Eve all things, except the fruit of this particular tree. However absurd it is, mankind fell for it. We should consider this when we are faced with temptations and when thoughts are planted in our minds that there is something that we just cannot do without.

When we consider all the things that Christ has freely given to us, such as happiness, our health, gifts, talents, and purpose, we should focus less on the things that are forbidden and more on the things that are made available to us. In order to be successful in this thought process, it requires that we maintain a posture of prayer. Thankfully, Christ was resurrected from the dead and then ascended to heaven. He then sent the Holy Spirit back to earth to provide comfort and strength for those that would receive. Henceforth, we can rely on the sustaining power of the Holy Spirit so that we will not fulfill the lusts of our flesh. We do not have to rely on our own strength because Christ has provided the power for us.

But you shall receive power when the
Holy Spirit has come upon you.
Acts 1:8a, NKJV

Prayer and Accountability

The keys to properly prepare for the next season of our lives include maintaining a consistent and healthy prayer life and by remaining connected to those who can help us to improve in areas in which we may fall short. Everyone needs one or two friends who can tell us the truth in love, even if it hurts. If we are isolated and cannot receive correction, then we will go through life believing that we have no flaws and will continually place blame for our failures upon other people.

We must take responsibility for our shortcomings and ask God to help us in areas of weakness. Maybe you have a temper or tend to be rude. Perhaps you have selfish ways or are inconsiderate. If we are sensitive to hear, then God will correct things within us during personal prayer, or He will speak to us through an individual. He will always give us loving correction in His Word; thus, we must study the Word of God so that it will take root in our hearts. A changed heart produces changed behavior. We must be willing to hear and receive correction and then take the proper steps to correct our behavior so that others can experience the love of Christ through us.

At one point in my life, I allowed so many things to rattle me and I would become upset. Through spending time with God in prayer and after talking to some accountability partners, I was able to adjust my temperament. In essence, I decided that I would not give away my power to opposing people or circumstances but would maintain my power by keeping my peace.

We have been given the perfect opportunity to maximize character development. Understand that character is developed in the presence of temptation.[29] Can you recall moments in your life in which you were faced with temptation, but you withstood it and maintained your integrity? Those are the milestones that we should strive for as singles so that if we desire marriage, we will not be novices in character development.

In this season, we must make certain to break behaviors and bad habits that were birthed out of seeds of despair. For instance, are you overeating nowadays? If so, did that behavior spring forth as a result of a disappointment? Are you a workaholic? Remember that we discussed how burying ourselves in other things such as work can be a means to cover our issues so that we can ignore them. If you sense that any of your habits or routines are as a result of some unfavorable circumstance, then seek the Lord on how you can release that subconscious burden and correct your behavior to reflect balance and your Kingdom identity.

Remember the discussion of Joseph from Training Day 3? When he was sold into slavery and began working at his master's house, he had been tempted several times by his master's wife to engage in sexual relations with her. Yet, he maintained his integrity and did not give in to the temptation. We ought to be committed to doing things God's way.

Recall that Adam and Eve's son Cain chose to do things his own way when he brought his sacrifice to God. He did not bring a sacrifice in humility and faith. He then got mad at his brother Abel because God favored him. It is dangerous to cut corners or to attempt to find avenues of compromise. God will always reward us when we strive to do our very best to please Him.

We must make a concerted effort to stay close to God in prayer and maintain accountability so that we do not create unnecessary detours for our future, especially when children are involved. This is a time in which we should invest in ourselves and work on areas of weakness, such as being more patient with ourselves and others. (People that are hard on themselves have a tendency to be hard on others.)

God may use you as an instrument to bring forth healing into someone else's life.

There are so many things that we are able to do in this season to enhance and invest in ourselves. For example, we can learn to forgive ourselves for past mistakes. We can then shift and learn to save money and invest in real estate or the stock market. Take the time to learn a new skill or pick up a new hobby. I challenge you to do something (wholesome) this year that you have been afraid to do. Live out loud!

At times, I may even set out to do too many things because I am so excited about the opportunities that are available to me in this season. This is the time in which we are able to paint with broad strokes on a brand-new canvas. You have the power to make your masterpiece beautiful. You can write your own song. Make it sweet.

If you desire a mate as I do, then we must continue to exercise patience. Consider how Ruth had become a widow, yet she chose to follow her mother-in-law back to Bethlehem and ended up marrying Boaz. They brought forth instrumental people that were a part of the lineage of Jesus. We must recognize that our decisions not only affect us, but they can affect other generations.

As mentioned previously, we are to engage in servanthood as we wait on the manifestation of the promises of God. Being single is not a means by which to glorify oneself, but it is a golden opportunity to perfect oneself. Serving God with our whole hearts will cause us to have more compassion upon others. This will help us in being true servants and lovers to our spouses if we desire marriage.

I once preached a sermon entitled, "The Struggle is Real, But Not Impossible!" Yes, we struggle as Christian singles, but we are overcomers through Jesus Christ. We do not have to rely on our own strength. By utilizing each of the aforementioned training tools, we will be more equipped to live victoriously during the single season and we will totally rock in our next! You can do this! We can do this!

Training Day 10

Stronger Than You Think

Regardless of where you were mentally, emotionally or spiritually on the day you began reading this book, today, you are stronger than you realize. Despite all the circumstances that have punched you and knocked you down, you have found a way to wake up each morning and keep going. You are stronger than you think.

Whenever a trainer completes a training program, he or she will assess where the client was at the beginning of the program and compare those statistics to the ending results. As mentioned on Training Day 1, boxing training programs are effective in that they are extensive in improving agility, core strength, cardio endurance, and technical skills. The individual components of the program are combined to render superior physical fitness, as well as offensive and defensive techniques that would make one a noteworthy boxing contender.

Sometimes while training, it may feel as though the tasks are too great in order to achieve the desired results. It may also feel as though some of the exercises are totally unnecessary and unrelated to effective boxing, just as I hated cardio training during off-season basketball practice. Yet, each day that one shows up to train, he is becoming stronger and more equipped for battle. Over time, he will have surpassed his own expectations. His body will have transformed, and his mind will be elevated to become keener and more proficient in anticipating the opponents' moves during competition.

Consider that when David was herding sheep, God was preparing him to reign over His people. David could not despise the day of small things, but he had to embrace it. When the curtain was pulled, David was prepared and was able to slay the giant Philistine. Imagine if David would have goofed around and had not taken his herding job seriously. He would not have been able to kill Goliath and there is a likelihood that many lives would have been lost at the hands of Goliath. Training season is crucial because if any essential skills are missing at the time of a fight, then it will affect a boxer's entire performance.

When Rocky Balboa was in Russia, he jogged through the knee-high snow, chopped firewood, climbed to the top of the mountain and he finally hit the punching bag. He seemed to be at a great disadvantage, but because of his will to push, he found a way to make the best out of unfavorable circumstances. Despite the Russian's size and illegal drug use, Rocky found a way to win. He was stronger than he realized. The one advantage that we have that Rocky did not have is that our fight has already been fixed! Christ has gone before us and has defeated every sickness, disease, failure, unfair advantage and, yes, heartbreak.

This compilation of concepts to defeat heartbreak and live in freedom while single is not exclusive, but it has worked for me. Each of the stages that I have shared are ones that I have employed in my personal life and continue to abide by daily. Take comfort in knowing that Christ has already won the victory and has borne the pain of your aching heart. Our job is to bring our lives into alignment with what Christ has already done for us through His redemptive work. We bring our lives into alignment with Him when we implement the following Kingdom strategies:

- Accept that Christ has already provided healing for our hearts through His redemptive work.

- Understand that sin is the cause of calamity in the earth, but that Christ has given us victory over every seemingly unfavorable circumstance.

- Get naked before God by being honest and transparent with Him about how we feel.

- Once we have expressed our feelings, we must beware of disappointment so that it does not linger and transform into discouragement.

- Stay focused on God and what He is doing in our lives, and look forward to His promises being manifested, shutting out all distractions.

- Fan the flame of faith by studying what God's Word says so that we may use Kingdom currency to access the promises of God, while fertilizing our soil by speaking His Word.

- Discover and sink ourselves into Kingdom purpose so that we can experience optimum self-fulfillment.

- Receive the oil of joy for sadness that is freely given so that we can live a life abundant in joy, creating a daily atmosphere of happiness.

- Prepare for the next season of our lives by fine tuning our character and by allowing God to transform our hearts to look like His.

I believe that these tools will be essential in your life as a single believer and they will be transferable tools in the next seasons of your life. Remember that we are heirs of God and joint heirs with Christ, so that makes us conquerors in every season and circumstance. No matter what it looks like, we win!

The Last Punch

I'd like to leave you with this last word. A pastor friend of mine shared a story of a young boy who had only one arm. He wanted to be a kickboxer so desperately, but no one would train him because of his condition. Kickboxing is a little different from traditional boxing because the fighters can use their feet. He sought trainer after trainer, but he was continuously turned down. Each coach would tell him, "Sorry, I will not be able to train you." So, the boy grew greatly discouraged and was ready to give up on his dream.

One day, he finally came across an elderly man at an old gym that happened to be a retired trainer. The old man agreed to train the young boy free of charge. He instructed the youngster, "Show up tomorrow and we'll get started training." So, as you would know, the young boy showed up to his first training class early and was eager to learn to be a kickboxer.

The old man gave the boy instructions and went over the rules of the sport. Then he gave him specific instructions on how to complete his first move. After a few tries, the youngster successfully completed the move. The old man expressed his approval and told the boy to return the next day for training.

The next day, the boy rushed in and was excited about the kickboxing move that he had just learned the day before. The old coach had the boy loosen his muscles and warm-up before beginning the session. After the warm-up, the coach instructed the lad to perform the move from the day before. The young boy did exactly as he was instructed. He performed this move several times until the old instructor told him, "Great job. Come back tomorrow." The boy was a bit confused and said, "Wait, aren't you going to teach me something else?" The man replied, "Come back tomorrow."

The next day was the third day of training. The routine was essentially the same. The young boy warmed up to loosen his muscles and then the coach had him to repeatedly execute the move he had learned two sessions prior. The boy was growing frustrated, but he just went with it. Finally, the instructor said it again. "Great job. Come back tomorrow." This went on for a total of 10 days. By the 10th day of training, the boy had perfected the one move that he had learned nine days prior.

The instructor told him, "Since you've gotten so good at perfecting this move, you're going to be in a tournament next week." The boy was excited, but thoroughly confused as he proclaimed, "I've always wanted to compete, but you've only taught me one move! There's no way I can defeat these guys with this one move!" The coach assured the youngster that all he asked was that he give it his best shot and that he would be proud of him no matter the outcome.

At the tournament, the young fresh fighter was excited and nervous. He had never competed in a tournament. He was fascinated by all the trophies he saw and all the people in the audience. Then, he noticed that some of the people in the audience gawked at him because he had one arm. Some of them whispered, "How is he going to fight with just one arm? Poor thing."

Finally, the boy's name was called for his first match. He told his coach, "He's too big. I don't think I can beat him." The coach assured him, "Just do what you've been trained to do." So, the young boy competed in his first match and performed the one and only move he was taught. It was a miracle! The rookie fighter won his first match and advanced to the second round. He couldn't believe it! The crowd roared in amazement.

When the bell rang for the second match, the young fellow noticed that this opponent was a little bigger than the first one. He told the trainer that he believed that he should just bow out gracefully and skip the match. The trainer would not allow it. So, the youngster toughed it out and did as he was told. He executed the move that he had learned in training and won round two! He could not believe it. He began to ask his trainer if the matches were rigged, but the trainer assured him that they were not. Since he had made it past rounds one and two, he would move on to the third round.

The young fellow took a short break and then the bell rang for round three. He said to himself, "I suppose I will just do the one move because my trainer didn't say to do anything else so far." His opponent came out, very cocky and arrogant, similar to Rocky Balboa's Russian opponent. The boy did his move and the crowd erupted in a roar! He was in utter disbelief that he had won round three and would move to round four, the championship!

Fighting in the championship match was a dream come true. When the young fighter was preparing for the title match, he felt a little more confidence. Except, his heart sank when he saw this opponent. He was even bigger than the last one. He asked his trainer for assurance. "Are you sure that there isn't something else that you should be teaching me so that I can beat this guy?" The trainer assured the young boy that he just needed to execute his move and he would be proud of him regardless of the outcome of the match.

The bell rang for the championship bout and the youngster got on his post. He was feeling anxious as he watched his opponent come toward him. At that moment, the trainer yelled out, "Do your move!" When the boy heard this, he performed the same move that he had learned just days prior in training. It was another miracle! The boy defeated his opponent and became the kickboxing champion! The audience erupted in amazement that this no-named, one-armed kid would walk away with the championship trophy!

On the way out of the gymnasium, the boy looked at his trainer and asked how he knew that he would win the tournament. The boy had no idea what the trainer was about to reveal to him. The old trainer stopped and looked the boy in the eyes. He stated, "I trained you for 10 days so you could perfect your craft. The training days became more intense and were equivalent to you winning the four rounds in the kickboxing tournament. I know you were discouraged because I only taught you one move. But you learned and mastered the most difficult move in the history of kickboxing. Plus, the only way to defend this particular move would require your opponent to grab your right arm in mid-air!"

> **Fighting in the championship match was a dream come true.**

After hearing the explanation, the boy stood there with his mouth wide open and began to shed a tear. All that time, he believed that he was at a disadvantage because he had a missing arm. Despite this, his greatest feat became his greatest attribute. The boy only had one arm and it was NOT the right arm!

This boy had gone through life believing that he was defeated and would never win any kickboxing tournaments. He had been turned away by other trainers because he appeared to be inadequate. Yet, when heaven and earth collided, he made contact with just the right person that could see his potential and know that he was literally built to win.

My friends, sometimes as singles, we may feel that we are inadequate or that we are at a distinct disadvantage in life. Nevertheless, God has given us all things that pertain to life and godliness and He has equipped us with power to do great exploits in the earth. We may be different from some of those around us because of our single status, but we are not outcasts, neither are we handicapped. We are equipped with the supernatural favor and Grace of God to win in the face of adversity. He created us to win!

Do not believe the lies that you are inadequate or less than others because you do not have someone attached to you in this season, such as a companion or spouse. Just like the young boy, you may have doubted yourself, your desirability, your calling, or your purpose. You may have felt that you have been dealt a poor hand in life. However, like the old instructor, I am here to advise you that you are a winner!

Notice that the young boy did not brush his desires to be a kickboxer under the rug. He kept pursuing his dreams. He did not say, "Well, I guess I have to wait until I can afford a

> **We are equipped with the supernatural favor and Grace of God to win in the face of adversity.**

prosthetic arm." No. He had the tenacity to win with the hand that he had been dealt. (No pun intended here.)

What is it that you desire to accomplish but you have not because you are waiting on a relationship or marriage? What gift is it that once burned deep within that you have allowed to lay dormant? Do not delay any longer. You must pursue your destiny and be all that God has called you to be in this single season. When you pursue your purpose, you will experience true fulfillment that cannot be shaken. It's time to take the stance of a winner. It's time for a knockout!

Keep using the moves and techniques that you have been taught throughout this book. Don't forget the lessons we have covered on each training day. Keep it as a reference point so that you can perfect your techniques just as the young fighter did.

Even if it seems that the techniques that you have learned aren't enough, keep doing them. It may seem redundant but keep going for His Grace is sufficient for you, and His power is made perfect in times of weakness. Like the old instructor, I say to you, "Do your move!" When it seems that you are up against a Goliath-like situation, "Do your move!" When loneliness attempts to creep back in, remember your training and "Do your move!" When the enemy brings discouragement, "Do your move!"

Listen to the Holy Spirit and He will guide you and may give you additional strategies to walk in freedom and fulfillment while living single. Be prepared for challenges after you have made a declaration that heartbreak has been defeated and cannot reign over your life. You will also be faced with tests in which the enemy will seek to prevent you from living in self-fulfillment. I implore you: do not faint. Do not stop here. If you should fall, repent and ask God for an abundance of His Grace, which is His divine enablement, so that you may continue to walk out the path that He has set before you.

"Don't you realize that in a race everyone runs, but only one person gets the prize? So run to win! All athletes are disciplined in their training. They do it to win a prize that will fade away, but we do it for an eternal prize. So I run with purpose with every step. I am not just shadowboxing. I discipline my body like an athlete, training it to do what it should" (I Corinthians 9:24–27a, NLT).

Early on I told you that at the end of a training program, a trainer will assess his or her clients' progress and end results. Thank you for sticking it out with me. My assessment is that you have the skill, the agility, the stamina and the strength to live like the champion that Christ has called you to be. You are a champion! Brothers and sisters, you are still here; you are stronger than you think!

It is my sincere prayer that you have accepted that you have the victory over heartbreak and every setback, that you understand how to live a life of purpose and genuine fulfillment, and that you will continue to grow **Stronger Every SINGLE Day**, and beyond!

Grace and peace be multiplied unto you.

Endnotes

1   Jordan, B., & Herrera, J. (2008). Medical Aspects of Boxing Musculoskeletal Medicine (2nd ed.): USA, IL: Humana Press.

2   EL-ASHKER, S. (2018). The impact of a boxing training program on physical fitness and technical performance effectiveness. *Journal of Physical Education & Sport, 18*(2), 926–932. Retrieved from https://search-ebscohost-com.libproxy.saumag.edu/login.aspx ?direct=true&db=s3h&AN=130654918&site=eds-live&scope=site

3   Schub, T. B., & Avital, O. R. B. M. (2018). Heart Failure: Psychological Factors. CINAHL Nursing Guide. Retrieved from https://search-ebscohost-com.libproxy.saumag.edu/login.aspx ?direct=true&db=nup&AN=T703169&site=eds-live&scope=site

4   Shen, B.-J., Xu, Y., & Eisenberg, S. (2017). Psychosocial and Physiological Predictors of Mortality in Patients of Heart Failure: Independent Effects of Marital Status and C-Reactive Protein. International Journal of Behavioral Medicine, 24(1), 83–91. Retrieved from https://search-ebscohost-com.libproxy.saumag.edu/login.aspx ?direct=true&db=s3h&AN=121061121&site=eds-live&scope=site

5   Miller, J. (2014). 25 Ways to prepare for marriage other than dating. Oklahoma: Miller Media & Communications.

6   The heavenly setting indicates that these are angels. Satan had come to oppose God's work.

7   Howard, J. (2010). HCSB study bible. Nashville: Holman Bible Publishers.

8   Id.

9   Consult a physician before beginning any workout regimen.

10 Leeming, S. J. (2009). Sigmund Freud, 1856–1939. Sigmund Freud (ELL), 1. Retrieved from https://search-ebscohost-com.libproxy.saumag.edu/login.aspx?direct=true&db=elr&AN=33551985&site=eds-live&scope=site

11 Id.

12 Zechowski, C. (2017). Theory of drives and emotions—from sigmund freud to jaak panskepp. Psychiat. Pol. *51*(6), 1181–1189.

13 Id.

14 Zellner MR, Watt DF, Solms M, Panksepp J. Affective neuroscientific and neuropsychoanalytic approaches to two intractable psychiatric problems: Why depression feels so bad and what addicts really want. Neurosci. Biobehav. Rev. 2011; 35(9): 2000–2008.

15 Copeland, G. "How Faith and Love are Connected." Retrieved from https://www.kcm.org/real-help/faith/learn/how-are-faith-and-love-connected.

16 Strong, J., Kohelenberger, J., & Swanson, J. (2001). The strongest strong's exhaustive concordance of the bible. Grand Rapids: Zondervan.

17 The Book of Daniel Chapter 10. NLT.

18 Benson, J. *Benson Commentary*. 1857. New York: T. Carlton & J. Porter. Retrieved from https://biblehub.com/commentaries/benson/.

19 "Grass and Grass Seed." Retrieved from https://www.scotts.com.

20 Montgomery, Steven. (2011). People patterns. (2nd ed.) Del Mar: Archer Books.

21 Nelson, D. & Quick, J. (2016). Organizational behavior. (5th ed.) Boston: Cengage Learning.

22 Id.

23 Rice, K. E. (2018). More on Maslow. Psychologist, 6. Retrieved from https://search-ebscohost-com.libproxy.saumag.edu/login.aspx ?direct=true&db=a9h&AN=131605058&site=eds-live&scope=site

24 Strong, J., Kohelenberger, J., & Swanson, J. (2001). The strongest strong's exhaustive concordance of the bible. Grand Rapids: Zondervan.

25 Howard, J. (2010). HCSB study bible. Nashville: Holman Bible Publishers.

26 Id.

27 Dake, F. (2001). Dake's annotated reference bible. Lawrenceville: Dake Publishing, Inc.

28 Merriam-Webster

29 McGee, J. (1981). Thru the bible. Nashville: Thomas Nelson, Inc.